The Salvation
of
La Purísima

T.M. Spooner

Floricanto Press

ISBN: 978-0-915745-88-3
Floricanto Press
650 Castro Street, Suite 120-331
Mountain View, California 94041-2055
www.floricantopress.com

"I'm going a long way off, Father, that's why I've come to let you know."

"And where are you going, if one may ask?"

"I'm going up North."

"And why up there? Don't you have your business here? Aren't you still in the pig-buying business?"

"I was. But not any more. It doesn't bring in anything. Last week we didn't make enough to eat and the week before we ate pure weeds. We're hungry, Father;..."

From the short story *Paso del Norte*. In *The Burning Plain and Other Stories* – Juan Rulfo

I

I was an outsider. My profession insisted upon it. And truthfully, many like-minded people might argue that is how it should have remained.

Huddled in a patch of trampled grass surrounded by a sea of burgeoning cherry trees, I sat with a group of Mexican migrant workers. We rested in one of the sprawling orchards of northern Michigan and as my profession demanded, I simply listened and chronicled. A documenter's journal rested on my lap, capturing empirical relevance in hastily scribbled notes. An equally intentioned cassette recorder spooled beside me. But as I rested in that careless circle of men, nearly one of them, yet something different, I felt lured by their lives. I was drawn by their words, rich descriptions, and in particular, of a tragedy that befell one of them. Or should I say to one of us? You see it was that way with my work. A fine gray line separated my scholarly responsibilities from what I will call Life.

We gathered in a crude circle and one by one each man explained how he had journeyed from Mexico to the United States. Each took his turn to recount in detail how he had left his home, his village, and crossed the vast desert or Río Grande. When one spoke, the others were quiet, granting respect and allowing each man the time to tell it, however he wished, in his own way. Honestly, many of the stories were similar and monotonous. But when Germán spoke his eyes grew thin and serious and his Adam's apple bobbed like a rubber ball trapped in his throat. The other men listened attentively. Germán's story was different. A man had died during his journey. The others knew of that possibility, but here was the detailed evidence. I set my pen down.

Although I listened intently to Germán, I couldn't relate as the others did. I could imagine and conjure up an imperfect image, but couldn't begin to see and feel it as they did: the gritty taste of the border, the heat and aridity, the air's peculiar scents, and the vision of the other side as unpromising as where they stood. It is true that there are things that we just can't know without experiencing. I hung on each of Germán's words.

"We were told of a place along the river that was narrow and where the water was shallow," he began. "A place where *la migra* seldom patrolled and where a man could walk across without getting his feet wet. It was easy, they said – almost too easy. But nothing ever is."

When he said that, several of the men, in mutual understanding, let out nervous laughter. He went on.

"It had been raining hard. It rained all the way from Michoacán, a steady downpour all through central Mexico. But when we neared the border it was only the hot desert. We should have known. We were ignorant I suppose. Ignorant to believe there was an easy way. Though three of us had done it before. There were four of us when we started, Jesús, Benito, Martín, and I. But

God didn't want us all to make it. Or maybe it was just that the river was out of God's reach. I used to believe that nothing was out of His reach. I don't believe that anymore."

Frequently, as he spoke, Germán caressed the top of his head. His hair was cut very short and the top must have felt like a wire brush. Two large black eyes suspended under bushy eyebrows of the same color, and one wrinkle jogged across the length of his forehead. He was angry with God.

"When we reached the river we found the current was fast. We walked along the bank for a long time. It was May and very hot. We searched for a narrowing in the river, but it never came. We were thirsty and had run out of water. Finally, we gave in and decided to cross where we were." I felt awkward for asking, but did anyway.

"Did you consider not crossing? Or waiting until the water had receded?" All of the men shook their heads. They all knew.

"Never, *maestro*," they answered in unison. They called me *maestro*, the Spanish word for teacher. It rolled off their tongues much easier than my given name, Paul Westin.

"We couldn't turn back," they all said. "So many had gone before us and this was our fate. Returning to La Purísima would have made cowards of us all. We had to cross, it's our duty."

Germán went on to reveal how four men had started across the river. He described the water as the color of *café con leche* and fierce in places. While they readied on the Mexican bank the men watched warily as a bloated cow carcass floated past. They managed to find a section that appeared less threatening and began. Germán went first to lead the others.

On the U.S. side a tree had fallen and a long branch, their lifeline, stretched far from the other bank.

"If we can just get to that branch it will guide us to the safety of the other side," Germán told them, "to the safety of the North."

Germán was not a born leader and in the past had shrunk from such responsibility. But clearly, he was the leader now and as soon as he had made that known became responsible for the others. At least in part, for he made the decision of where to cross and called on them to follow.

He called to the others with newfound confidence. Two of the men said silent prayers and Germán watched Jesús cross himself before descending from the bank and slipping into the water. They had nothing but the clothes on their backs. Others in the town who had gone before advised them to take nothing.

"For sure it will be lost," they had said. "Or worse, it will survive and then only be a painful reminder of home. Better to forget, at least for a while." The men accepted the advice.

Germán started slowly and cautiously, like walking a high wire, his arms stretched wide for balance. Beneath the water's surface the force of the current was strong and he struggled against the invisible tugging force. It wrapped itself around his ankles like a snake, an evil spirit with deadly intent.

"There were moments when I was sure I'd be washed away," he said. "I'm a strong swimmer, but no challenge for that whipping current. I went carefully and every ounce of my strength was used. It took everything I had to reach that hanging branch. I thanked God when I reached it, but soon wished I hadn't. Thanked Him for what?"

Germán called to Jesús to start out. Jesús was older than Germán, somewhere in his thirties, strong and serious. As Jesús set out he thought of his two sons. They were seven and four. Germán made his way up the bank on the other side –the side that promised something better. But here along the river both sides looked the same.

"If you glanced up and down both sides like I did, you couldn't tell which side belonged to whom," Germán said sadly. "I couldn't tell the feel of my own country— my Mexico. I thought I would always know. I searched the other shore and saw my friends, the other men, all of us children of Mexico who are unable to survive in our own land. We are deserters in a sense – but so are so many others. All of the struggles just for the chance to pick cherries in Michigan. A chance to earn a living and join the rest of the men from La Purísima and all the other small towns in Mexico."

Jesús followed, granting faith in the leader. Germán continued his story.

"Jesús took my steps. Somehow he found them in the muddy river bottom. He reached the bank on the side of promise and I lent my hand and pulled him up to dry land. Then two remained. They were brothers: Benito and Martín. Neither wanted to be the last to cross. Both were afraid and Martín never wanted to come north, but had to. Benito was older so he went first." Germán spoke with a trace of emotion now. "It was the last thing he ever did."

Germán grew more solemn and serious. He stared at the orchard's grassy earth under the shade of a cherry tree and relived what happened next.

Benito eased to the bank. When he did the earth shuffled at his feet. On the U. S. side of the river, Germán and Jesús drifted away from the bank. The banks were crumbling. Dirt and mud slid into the river. Benito was in the water. It was higher than when Germán had gone, nearly reaching Benito's waist. They all sensed the danger. Across the river, on the Mexican side, the bank just upstream from Benito collapsed. In an instant, Benito was swept under. The bank's thick muck poured into the river, quickly shifting the current. The current, which felt like a snake around Germán ankles, tightened around Benito's.

Germán paused to compose himself. We understood what had happened. Benito had drowned in the river. The men, two on the north side and the other still on the Mexican bank, ran along shouting at the chocolate abyss of swirling and snarling water. They never saw another sign of Benito.

"And then we just stood there, dazed, and we stared back across to Mexico. Back to that barren place of desert and shrubs. But it was the same where we stood. It looked no different. Benito's young brother, Martín, was frozen. He stood there, as dumb as we were, with his mouth dropped open and eyes wide. You couldn't hear. All our thoughts were buried in the violent rush of the river—the river that never stops. It wouldn't stop for Benito."

As I listened I thought how my world had never encountered such tragedy. But I learned that these men's lives are riddled with it. In their minds, a life without it is not complete. It isn't full. It must possess potholes and caverns to trap somber and sullen memories. I glanced around the circle of men and studied their faces, understanding how economics and social coercion pulled them north. They knew more of Life than I did. They knew of struggle and survival. I knew nothing of either.

The full and slow moving clouds cast oblong shadows over the orchard. I brushed a beetle off my notepad and gazed above at slim shreds of blue sky. One of the men had loosened a small stone from the hard earth and tossed it into the distance. The muffled impact set off a flock of starlings, their wings beating heavily in the early summer air.

"And what about Martín?" I asked. "Did he cross?" Germán shook his head and answered.

"No, Jesús and I stared at him for a long time. Then I thought we must make him cross. We couldn't just leave him there. I can still see the fear in his face. We had to finish what we had set out to do, even if only three of us would make it."

Germán had waved for Martín to cross. His brother was gone. He had to forget that now. Germán called to him, shouting above the roar of the river. Martín would have plenty of time to grieve later.

"What else could we do? God was of no help," Germán said.

But Martín couldn't hear with the sound of the river. He only shook his head and then ran along the bank—back and forth in a kind of rage or torment like a caged animal. He shouted to the others, but they couldn't hear him. Germán went on.

"Martín stared across at us. 'No!' We read the words

on his lips. He turned and ran back into the arms of his country. The country that didn't want him and offered nothing to go back to. We never saw him again. Then I wished I had never given thanks when I reached the other bank. Thanks for what! We were only two then. That's my story."

The men were quiet and soon began to rise and return to work. Wherever men gather a sense of slowness or boredom lingers, and movement is subdued. The mind recalls broken dreams, and a lazy, sluggish pace. The dreams of youth seem so far away, dispersed into a dark night, or worse, slipped away in broad daylight on a cloudless, sun filled day, when weariness in a circle or long line of men replaces ambition and drive.

I gathered my notebook and cassette recorder; the others went their way. They disbanded in twos and threes, off into the orchard or back to the little shacks where they boarded during the picking season. Germán walked alone toward the thickness of the orchard. The cherries were ready and any day the harvest would begin. The globes of red with long stems, now hanging heavy, were easy to pick. I snatched one from a nearby tree and tasted it, grimacing at its tartness. My car waited in the gravel nearby. If I left now I would make it back to Chicago before dark.

II

Graduate school students are riddled with insecurities. I was a doctoral student at the University of Chicago. For the past six months I had been working on my dissertation – a study of Mexican immigrants laboring in the cherry orchards of northern Michigan. The Traverse Bay region is the heart of the country's tart cherry industry. The study had required several trips to Michigan over the past months.

"It must be a labor of love," my mentor and doctoral sponsor had told me. Professor René Lassene, a French Canadian from Quebec, was the reason I had pursued anthropology. When I had taken one of his courses sophomore year I longed to be just like him – knowledgeable and worldly. He was a man who understood cultures and histories as they were – man made.

What the professor lacked in physical stature, he was no more than five feet seven inches tall, he more than compensated for in knowledge. He had traveled widely and conducted fieldwork all over the world. His earliest field experience was in the tiny African country of Rwanda in the 1960s. Sub-Saharan Africa, especially Rwanda, became his area of specialty. He spoke the primary language of the country, Kinyarwanda, and held a vast and deep understanding of both the Hutu and Tutsi people. He talked about going back, but he was getting up in years and would retire in another year. The genocide of 1994 had deeply saddened him. Professor Lassene had taught me the craft. I had done field studies in the Andean region of Peru and also in the Mexican state of Oaxaca. Fortunately, by now, I spoke Spanish well.

"It's much more than statistics," the professor would say. "You must gain the trust of the people and in a sense become one of them. Gaining their trust is the most important aspect and the most rewarding. But never lose sight of your profession."

Over the past months I had gotten to know several of the men working in the cherry orchards. Germán Medina was the one I had grown closest to. He came from a village called La Purísima in the agrarian state of Michoacán, Mexico. Nearly all of the men at the orchard came from the same village in Michoacán. During the picking season La Purísima is reduced to women, children, and the elderly. Coming to Michigan to pick had become not only a means for economic survival, but also a rite of passage for the young men—a passage into the throes of manhood. I thought of Germán's story about the crossing and what had become of Martín. How had he made his passage?

It was dark when I returned to Chicago. The night was clear and the glow of the city's lights made it look strange, almost unreal. My apartment was close to the university in Hyde Park. Jennifer, my fiancée, had expected me back earlier. I would have to call to let her know that I wouldn't see her tonight. When I arrived at the apartment I called, but she wasn't at home. I left a message assuming she was out with co-workers. She worked at an advertising agency. I never had the stomach for her co-workers, or she for my anthropology colleagues for that matter. Many times I thought we made a strange couple. She would say, "I don't know how you can tolerate *those* people." She accentuated the word those, as if they were lepers or something other than human. Jennifer would never understand my passion.

I heated water for tea and reviewed the scribbled notes from the day. The cassette tape was still in the player and I rewound it. With the steaming teacup cradled in my hands I listened again to Germán's story. It was difficult to understand what risks these men take in order to work for a few months. I had to understand. It may be more than harsh economics, I thought— something more than sheer survival. What had developed, at least in La Purísima, was that the transit into manhood had changed. It was defined now by the ceremonial crossing to the North—a successful passage to the North.

Again I thought of Martín. A country like Mexico, steeped in the myth of machismo, may not be forgiving or understanding of a young man who turned his back. I listened to Germán's recorded voice and let the words wash over me. I listened to where his voice trembled and what he had said about wishing he hadn't thanked God. His voice was unsteady, shifting, then pausing, high and low, rambling at times as he relived those nightmarish moments at the river. Soon the voice was drowned out by fatigue. I fell asleep on the couch with the cassette player still turning, Germán's captured voice still explaining.

* * *

A weekly visit to Professor Lassene's office was like a trip into antiquity. His office was cradled with bookshelves. His heavy desk was placed in the center and a comfortably worn leather chair was pushed into the corner. A bold-colored blanket he had used in Africa was draped behind the back of his chair. An African motif defined the room; masks of Tutsi Kings hung on the walls, Old World maps, fierce looking warrior heads, and faces of mythical creatures filled the room. Dark drapes, pulled shut, trapped the dark and the scent of musk and age, as if the light would arouse the resting creatures best left to a listless and weary past.

In Professor Lassene's office one would never know if it were day or night, winter or summer. It was as if time and the seasons were irrelevant. Professor Lassene sat at his desk, tiny behind the thick wood. He wore silver-framed glasses and had a tiny gray mustache. I leaned back in the leather chair in the shadowy corner as he inquired about the progress of my dissertation.

"Coming together," I said. "I've gathered statistics on the numbers of immigrants to the region and the number of pickers in the industry."

"Assimilation?" he asked.

"None to speak of. These men are separate and wish to remain that way. They're temporary workers who will return to their homes." I told the professor of the town in Michoacán called La Purísima. It seemed the entire crop of village males were in Michigan.

"What are the effects on the community?" he asked. "On the families left behind during the harvest? The women? The children?"

I hadn't considered all of this yet, I told him, a little embarrassed.

"Perhaps you should go to La Purísima," he suggested. "To witness first hand the impact and change for the community. A complete analysis."

I thought it would perhaps be a good idea and said so. But I filed the idea away, not truly taking it seriously at the time. In truth, I didn't feel it was necessary for my project and could get away without it.

The professor looked frail, almost feeble behind the massive mahogany desk. I had never fully acknowledged it until now, but my mentor's academic career would soon end. Perhaps I couldn't let myself accept it since he had long been my reason for this passion. His life now was subdued and at times he seemed weary of it all and perhaps he was ready to leave it behind him. Yet somehow I sensed he still possessed some vigor for the profession. And any studies I conducted, in a sense, we conducted.

At moments, in the center of those gray pale eyes, brightness called and youthful eagerness and energy cried out. I would be the last doctoral candidate he sponsored. For that I felt pride, and understood that a final run, though vicariously, was perhaps what he yearned for. He no longer spent time in the field. His place was in an armchair surrounded by antiquities and photographs of Africa. I found him in one photograph on the bookshelf, in a long row of dark colored men, yet there was no contrast between them. His pale skin, kept so long from the sun in his Quebecian youth, did not betray his African comrades and they seemed to blend as a single man, all like sons of Africa.

Professor Lassene taught me most that cultures are man made. Climate, economic necessity, and perhaps most of all, a universal urge for power defines them. What most intrigued Professor Lassene were those cultures considered less sophisticated than our own, like those in remote areas of the Amazon and others, like Rwanda in the 1960s. Here, one found a closer relationship with and knowledge of nature.

"We can only see in other cultures what it is we know and what we have experienced," he had said. "We're all ethnocentric and see only through prescription lenses, a correction that fits our own circumstances and our cultural identity. Not one of us was dropped from the sky by some alien bird. We were born somewhere, to someone. We've all come of age within a social and cultural structure, one that defines us no matter where we travel. We cannot escape the fact that in the end we are imperfect observers. We can never deny that."

I left the professor's office forgetting if it were day or evening. Denied light in his office always distorted my sense of time. I think that was his sly intention. After all, nothing ever is exactly as it appears. There was more research to do and I went to the library. I had time before the undergraduate class I taught in the afternoon.

The question of assimilation was trapped in my mind. I realized that for the cherry pickers there was no desire for it. The men simply wished to transplant their own culture, language, and everything that went with it into their small plot in Michigan. They weren't interested in the world of the Gringo. There was no desire to adopt any of his customs or habits, nor was there any desire to influence him in any way. These men had no intention of convincing or persuading the Anglo, the ruler of *Gringolandia*, of anything. They simply didn't care. And that logic is rational, for their work is seasonal and temporary and each man will eventually return to his village. He will pack up his language and the rest of it and go home. It made me think of a former professor and a story he had related to me about assimilation. He had spent many months in the Far East, primarily Taiwan.

"I knew I was adjusted, if not assimilated one day," he said, "when I noticed a strange looking man walking toward me on the streets of Taipei. His eyes were light and round; I quickly realized he was a foreigner – an Anglo, like me."

* * *

Jennifer was like a strong breeze. Sometimes she was an excessively strong breeze. Jennifer Cottard was still athletic and very active. She was twenty-six now and relentless about her career. The ambition and drive to win that was once directed at pursuits of volleyball and swimming, was now pointed firmly at a career in advertising. There was much more to gain now, she thought. For her it was primarily money, any excuse for sporadic snobbishness and selfishness. The truth was all that mattered so little to me.

Advertising seemed the work that best suited her. She had a way, undetectable to the victim, of persuading a person that they needed exactly what she was promoting. Even if the product was truly of no use to them. Though, I suppose that is the soul of advertising.

"The idea is to fool the masses," she would say. "Persuade them to purchase what they don't need, simply by convincing them that a product is a necessity or at best is such an object of envy that they must possess it." I understood the logic, but always felt there was something sinister about it.

Jennifer and I met that evening for dinner. Her discriminating palette craved Italian so we met at a restaurant specializing in the cuisine of Northern Italy.

"So late last night," she said almost sadly. "I missed you." We sat at a candlelit table neatly set for two. Her sleeveless blouse exposed her broad shoulders, that way from years of competitive swimming.

"It was," I agreed. "I stayed later than expected. I was mesmerized with the men's stories of their border crossings. Many of them are tragic. One man told of a drowning."

Jennifer sipped her wine and looked at me with droopy, deep blue eyes. Her face was round and it seemed she had hung onto a bit of baby fat, but that was part of her beauty and charm. She was what some might call wholesome, though she was fit and active. She had a tenacious way about her and an endless cache of energy. Undoubtedly, she was the smartest person I had ever known. She was not the most intelligent by any means, but the smartest. There is a distinct difference between the two. Jennifer had a sharp, quick way of learning things. She had a knack for striking the core despite troublesome peripheral complexities of ethics and such. Her method left no time for lingering over ideas or philosophies, but rather, honed in on what was worth knowing. And to her, that meant useful information, not necessarily knowledge.

On some level I admired this. For Jennifer, all that mattered was getting to the central point or idea and then swiftly moving to the next, like a honeybee skirting from flower to flower, unconcerned with color, botanical classification, or potential medicinal purposes. The name of the game was to extract the sweet nectar, only to move quickly to the next. Never linger more time than necessary despite the beauty or the secrets that might dwell there. She was smart, and above all, a pragmatist.

For me it was different. I was much more the beetle, lingering at points along a leafy stem or fanning petal. I would venture out on a thorn or droopy leaf simply to gather whatever useless knowledge I could. Perhaps arriving at the center was secondary to me. For me, the name of the game was contemplation, a lingering waltz, meandering gazes, and the hope of catching a gentle breeze on the underbelly of a luscious leaf. You might say I was the master of the superfluous.

Jennifer and I were very different. I liked to loiter and at times arriving at the end, like the end of a novel, was sad to me. For me the act of reading the words, like a rhythmic wash of golden waves, was all the enjoyment and value. For Jennifer reading meant getting to the end so she knew what happened. And for that reason literature annoyed her. I was forced to tell her, "in literature, seldom does something overtly happen. That's the difference between fiction and literature. Literature is less about what is said than how it is said." From then on she hated literature.

It was the same with a piece of music, like a Schubert trio or Puccini aria, and the melancholy I often found in the mournful, fading finish. But while I wandered Jennifer was far ahead, consumed with the liquid sustenance and a full belly of pragmatism. And so, she was a natural for the world of business, while for me, I was a natural for a scholarly world. As a couple then, we combined the best of both worlds, or so we had convinced ourselves.

"You look tired," she said as she reached across the table and gently caressed my cheek. I felt a shiver along the back of my neck and turned my head slightly and then sipped the wine. It was dry and tasted good.

"I spoke to my father today," she said. "The hotel ballroom is reserved for the wedding reception. Can you believe the wedding is only six months off?" she asked excitedly. "We have so much yet to do."

"No, I really can't," I said absently. "But everything will come together, Jen," I assured her. Her father, a cardiologist, and her mother, a lawyer, would insist that all plans were carried out to the letter.

"You seem preoccupied tonight," she said, noticing my attention drifting.

"Just thinking of work. There is still much to do for the dissertation. And the drowning I mentioned to you is eerie. I keep thinking about it."

"Oh, but afterward you will be a doctor," she cheered. "And then you can say goodbye to field studies. From there it will be a full professorship at Chicago," she predicted. "Everything you ever wanted."

"A full professorship surely won't happen overnight," I reminded her. "And you know field study will always be a part of my work."

Jennifer and I had discussed all of this before, in detail. However, her feelings about me "traipsing off to some Godless place," as she called it, just to study "strange" cultures simply turned her stomach. She preferred the academician, stuffed behind a cherry wood desk, dressed in a neat suit, imposing, and flashing the title of Doctor of Philosophy.

"Yes," she said, though she still denied the field studies. "But darling, I know you'll work around that. I really don't want you picking up some awful disease someplace."

"Don't worry," I said. "Besides, my dissertation takes me no further than Michigan. I'm not aware of any especially awful disease indigenous to Michigan."

During dinner we were interrupted twice—once by one of Jen's coworkers and another by a former client who was in town from Atlanta. It was storming and once the lights went out and a collective "ah" swallowed the place like an elementary school classroom. We finished dinner and spent the night at Jennifer's, but I couldn't forget Germán's story and the strange concern I had over the plight of Martín. It was one of those things that seep in over time. It affects one more after time has passed, like a delayed reaction, dismissed until it can be more fully absorbed or understood. That, after all, is the way of the beetle.

III

The following week I returned to Michigan. The cherry harvest had begun. On the way I drove through towns that hugged Lake Michigan, those sleepy towns with a sandy beach and public parking, and a lighthouse or two that attract tourists from Illinois and Ohio. And one town, called Holland, boasted an authentic windmill and a tulip festival in the spring.

Once I stopped in a town called South Haven, hoping to climb to the top of the lighthouse and peer out across the winking water to watch the sailboats. I walked to the end of the long peer to the bright red lighthouse, but was disappointed to find it locked. It was sealed up tight with a thick padlock and heavy chain. The wind was stiff that day and I walked barefoot for a time in the gray sand and scared off the gulls. Afterward I found a bench along the jetty and passed an hour watching sailboats coming in and out of dock. Each weekend sailor waved to me except for one boat with two young drunks, likely locals out on their father's boat. Between the passing boats, with sails down, I held a hand over my light eyes and searched the waters for boats in full, glorious sail. In the distance they were nothing but white specks on the horizon. The intense light hurt my eyes and the shimmer of the sun's rays on the water made me drunk and dizzy.

In town were small specialty shops. One in particular I recall was replete with everything to do with blueberries. There were candles, shirts, china, and more – all with the scent, shape, or image of blueberries. I've forgotten the name, though I found a blend of coffee that had blueberry ground in. I bought some and tried it later, not able to resist my curiosity and the heavy scent of berry in the place.

Further north I veered from the lake and cut slightly eastward toward the center of the state. And soon, drove straight north, anticipating the cherry orchards where I would find Germán and the other men. The area around Traverse City is known as the cherry capitol of the world. Michigan has some thirty-six thousand acres of cherry orchards.

The men would be hard at work now, from sun up until sundown, and the harvest's momentum and force would churn like a mechanical thing. The men could be the same or different from year to year. It didn't matter so long as the work was done. The men knew it too and used the landowner as much as he used them. It was a fine, reciprocal relationship. The men, already dark, grew darker under the midday's hot sun. June is when the cherry harvest takes place in northern Michigan and is finished by the end of the month. From the work, the men's hands stain bright red, like something violent had taken place.

I asked them if they wished to stay here permanently.

"For what? We have a McDonalds in Mexico." They laughed, feeling they had gotten one over on me.

"Yes," I said. "I suppose this culture doesn't much raise brows. The standard of living does."

That was it, they agreed.

"The idea is to earn money and return home. And God willing, we will be back next year for the harvest." I understood what they meant. The U.S. is driven by immediacy, while Mexico is driven by tradition. Immediacy versus boredom, or carelessness I suppose.

After parking my car I popped out quickly, eager to stretch my legs that had grown stiff during the long drive. I leaned my hands against the car door and pushed, my legs stretched and scratched at the tiny gravel stones at my feet making a patch of bare dirt. I had been thinking of Jen and wondered for the first time how this marriage might possibly work. It was not the kind of thought that should be running through your mind six months before the wedding.

A band of men was moving in the distance. They looked sluggish and tired, sufficiently beaten by work. But still, they smiled and their teeth shown white against their dark, ruddy faces. There was a hum of voices, a murmur from the swarm of men in hats and dark, stiff jeans. It was noontime and they were coming in for lunch. I called to one of the men I recognized and asked for Germán.

"He's coming, *maestro*!" he called back with a wave and then pointed to another small group of men behind his own. Then I noticed Germán's familiar gait in the distance.

For lunch the men would gather in small groups,

never a man alone, and sit or lie on the ground. They spread beans on tortillas and drank cola or Jarritos, a Mexican soft drink: tamarind, lime, or guava. It grew quiet while they ate. I often sat with them during the silent communion. Each time I sensed an inner voice within each of them. The silence siphoned from the reservoir of their personal past and from their country's dark and violent history—a collective weight that stirred deep within each of them. The men banded together, forming deceptive energy. Afterward, they would fall asleep, one by one, on the dry earth –the earth that they seemed so close to and familiar with. Some curled and hugged it like a down pillow or a rolled blanket, while others lined up stiff, like dark tipped matches.

"*Maestro*!" Germán shouted when he noticed me. "How is Chicago?" he asked as he drew near. I could see his full, black eyebrows.

"Still there," I said. "Waiting for you and Jesús."

"No, Jesús thinks there is evil in the city. The devil is in them all," Germán said. "After the harvest I will visit. But now, let's eat," he said, and I followed him and three other men to a shaded area under an elm tree.

We scattered about in the grass, still cool and protected by the tree leaves and branches. Although the men had little they never hesitated to share with me. I would graciously accept small amounts and would curiously fill up quickly. It was a delicate balance of accepting, but not exceeding. Germán filled a tortilla with beans, rolled it, and handed it to me.

"*Chile*?" he asked.

"Of course," I said knowingly and tipped the bottle and watched a few small drops of red liquid meet the beans. The other men, the ones I didn't know so well, watched intently. One of them studied me more suspiciously than the others.

"*Mas!*" he said to me. "*Mas chile!*" he urged. I motioned to him with my hand, a gesture I had learned from the men. It was a rapid flip of the back of my hand toward him, which meant no. It grew quiet as we ate. Soon the other men were resting. The one with his arms folded behind his head, the suspicious one, rested a Los Angeles Dodgers baseball cap over his face. It didn't appear they slept soundly. One part of them was asleep, but another, the fearful part remained awake, on guard whenever they slept in this Godless land.

One of the men once told me, "your country is Godless, *maestro.*"

"Why do you think so?" I asked him curiously.

"Because," he began, "your churches are new and modern, clean and shiny. But God is very old. In Mexico everything is old." He spoke seriously as if educating me. "And God is there, everywhere with us. You see?" It was quiet for a time and the man appeared to be in thought, maybe wrestling with his own simple logic. "But here it may be a different God," he finally said. "A new God. A new God of the gringos. Well, he said carelessly. "Who knows, *maestro*? Who knows...?"

I asked Germán about Martín and what had become of him.

"We never heard from him again. It's been more than a year. At least he's never returned to La Purísima. Some say he died in the desert. Dried up like a lizard on some stone. Others say he lives in the Sierra de Mil Cumbres of Michoacán as a recluse, never able to look into the eyes of another man."

"And what do you think?" I asked.

"I think he's alive—someplace in Mexico. Too full of grief and shame to face anyone."

Germán took a drink when one of the resting men spoke.

"I think he's dead. He's a ghost now," he said. It was the suspicious one, his face still hidden beneath the baseball cap. "A shamed ghost. And angry too. The worst kind."

"Why angry?" Germán quickly asked. The man didn't answer. "Angry at whom?" Germán asked again.

"Maybe at you," the man responded.

"Why at me?"

"You killed his brother, didn't you?" the faceless man asked, not stirring.

"No," Germán defended, as if to convince himself as much as the rest of us. "God killed him. Or maybe the devil—not me."

The lunch break had ended. It was time to return to work. The men rose slowly and started back to the orchard. They went, unthinking it seemed, without complaint or expression. Each man was in his own thoughts now. I left them and returned to the sanctuary of my own thoughts. I went into town for something to eat and to find a room for the night.

The hotel was on the main street. The façade was flat, built from reddish brick with a turquoise awning stuck out over the entire width of the sidewalk. The awning hung low in front forcing me to duck my head when I passed under it from the street. I had stayed here before, the other times when I spent a day or two near the orchards. There were shops along the street, though I had never ventured past the diner next door. I went in for a late lunch and took a table in the corner, out of the sun's reach. I ordered a BLT, the diner's specialty, and a Coke, also their specialty. They were short on variety, but it didn't matter for the stay would be brief. Besides, back in the city I had my pick of cuisine and variety was never a question. Here there was little room for confusion—a short list for everything.

The waitress was familiar. I had seen her before and was quite sure she remembered me too, though neither of us made it known. It's simpler that way I suppose. It's not necessary to feign anything more than congeniality. Hello, thank you, and good-bye would do. After lunch I went up to my room, took a shower, and then began making notes. I did some writing for the dissertation and worked for a couple of hours. After working I grew bored and took a short nap. There was a movie theater across the street from the hotel; I went over for the early show. During the movie I must have fallen asleep since I didn't follow the plot or else it was just loose. Afterward, I walked back across the street and turned in early.

The following day it rained steadily. The men worked early, but were forced to quit before noon because of the weather. I met with Germán in the small wooden building where he boarded. He shared the small space with Jesús, the other man he crossed the river with a year ago. Both men were there and they offered me a chair while each sat on his narrow bed.

"We make good study, no?" Jesús asked with a rare smile. I laughed at his comment and asked the reason for his light mood. Jesús Prado was generally a serious and stoic man. He was older than both Germán and me, married, and had two sons.

"I'm bringing my family," he said. "From Mexico. My wife and sons are coming." He called his sons *machitos,* and it was easy to read the pride on his face whenever he spoke of them.

"Where will they stay?" I asked him.

"We are getting an apartment," he responded happily. "It has one bedroom, but it will do. After the harvest I have a permanent factory job waiting. We will make a life here," he said with optimism.

Germán shook his head, almost in disgust. It was true that many men from Mexico worked in nearby factories.

Jesús began again excitedly, "and the *machitos* will go to school here. At least Samuel, he is seven now. Maybe the little one, Pepito, will wait. He is only four, but so smart for his age." Jesús smiled again widely. It must have pained his face since it was such a rare occurrence and the muscles could not be accustomed to such effort. His walnut colored skin had been still until now, smooth without mark or indention.

"The boys won't like an apartment," Germán commented. "Believe me. Look, they are used to the open fields and the air. You will learn," Germán said, stopping himself from further predictions.

Jesús shifted the attention to me. "And, what about you? Do you have a girlfriend, *maestro*? Or maybe a wife?"

"No wife yet, but I'm engaged." Jesús asked for her name. "Jennifer."

"She's pretty, no?" he asked.

"She is," I admitted. "And smart too. I think more smart than pretty."

Germán seemed more withdrawn now and serious. His head hung and his entire body drooped. As Jesús grew more animated and free, Germán seemed to withdraw further.

"And you, Germán?" I asked. "A girlfriend?"

"Yes," he answered, a little sadly. "Hortencia." He said her name and then sighed. It was a kind of surrendering sound, from deep within him.

"Do you miss her?"

"I do," he answered solemnly. "But this is temporary for me," he added. "I have no intention of staying past the harvest. I'm only here to earn money each year and I send nearly all of it home to my family. I don't like to be away from my home, or from Hortencia," he admitted. "For now though this is necessary."

"Economics can be cruel," I said. He nodded in agreement.

"But what's to miss?" asked Jesús. "There is nothing back there to miss — nothing to yearn for. Only a life of struggle and poverty."

"Yes, but poverty is not a crime," Germán pointed out.

"For me, I won't look back," Jesús said. "I will tell the *machitos* the same. Never look back — only ahead." He spoke confidently now. "And God willing, one day you will prosper. That is what I will tell them. Just don't look back over your shoulder. Never."

It rained the remainder of the afternoon. It came strong and then weakened, minimized to a patter, but never completely ceased. When we thought it had stopped it would come again, angrier. I spent the afternoon with Jesús and Germán listening to their stories of home and reluctantly sharing some of my own world.

There was no work that afternoon and of course no pay for the men. The thought of Martín and what had become of him was a silent, but constant hammering among us. We shared that now. It was now a distinct voice within us. And as men gather, our inner voice calls and taps at our consciousness. In my own head, I heard the far off murmur of a man, shamed and grief stricken. Either one of the two could drive a man mad. It seemed my rational and scholarly logic for a time was swayed, and myth and a surreal world of ghosts and supernatural mystery drifted through my mind like clouds. I was, after all, nothing but an observer.

"We can never escape that." I could hear Professor Lassene preaching or chanting like a mantra in his French-Canadian accent. Observation is the call and the common denominator for the anthropologist. It's a self-imposed limitation or constraint, but also our greatest tool for understanding. It's our fiercest weapon and our greatest defense. "Never forget," Professor Lassene had said.

It's true that if we forget the mantra we'll be destined to be swallowed by or own humanity, our own weaknesses. And then, our inquiry, our judgment and professionalism will be destroyed. What we see will be through weak and untrained eyes – subjective and judgmental. We won't see through the eyes of a trained scientist, the keen pupil of science.

"We are mere observers," the professor would say. If we forget, our analysis will reduce to what we see in others. I had told him once that we might become what we see in others. He corrected me.

"We are what we see in others. If we cross the line of our profession that's all we can see and we'll project our own values."

IV

As part of my work at the university, I taught a third-year cultural anthropology course. Although rare among my colleagues, I actually enjoyed teaching. But now my focus was on the dissertation and achieving my doctorate. Much of the earliest stages of the research were spent gathering data and then more data gathering. It took some time to identify an industry, but once I did, Michigan was the logical choice.

I had learned that during the harvest time La Purísima found itself without young men. The town consisted of the old, of women, and children. The older men assumed the work that was normally done by the young men. Many of them were very old and feeble. Germán and Jesús had told me that the old men, in their day, were never forced to leave their homes.

"If you went to La Purísima now," Jesús said, "you would see the old men on the backs of burros with large bunches of palm leaves beneath them. The saddle would be made of a bed of grasses with long lashes. And the men's looks are serious and strong and as long as the mountains. Because of us they must work. They are our fathers and grandfathers. Others who are too old sit under trees in the shade, or in front of their homes, watching the days pass. The main road of the town is only dirt, *maestro*. Not so much like here."

They told me the women get lonely and sometimes the nights become too dark and cold.

"That's when they miss us most. When there is a chill in the night air, especially after a rain. Oh, *maestro*, that's when we miss them most too," they confessed.

"They are the stronger sex," Jesús said. "Maybe they invent the loneliness just to make us feel wanted," he mused.

The town, La Purísima, is found along the edges of the Sierra de Mil Cumbres, a vast mountain range in the southeastern portion of Michoacán. The name means the mountains of a thousand peaks. La Purísima is about an hour and a half bus ride from the capital city of Morelia.

"I only go to the city when I have to," Jesús told me. "There is evil there, like in all big cities. I was forced to go there once in order to get my marriage license. I was young and frightened, but for my marriage it was worth the risk. I would do anything to be with my Dulce."

From what the men had told me there was no running water in many of the homes and only sporadic electricity. It was a half-hour bus ride from the main highway to La Purísima.

"Sometimes more," Jesús said. "If there is much rain, which there often is. And then the dirt road turns to mud and it's more work for the bus. Sometimes the bus gets stuck and other times the driver won't even bother to come to La Purísima. It's too far off the main highway. Then we're forced to walk to the highway. What else can we do, *maestro*?" he asked. "We are poor— we have no voice. It's different there, you know."

Germán was more modern than Jesús, in dress, in thought, and in everything. He had worked for a time in Morelia, in the central distribution center of the city. He loaded trucks with fruits from all over Mexico: papayas, mangos, oranges, melons, grapefruit...

"Evil is not only in the cities," Germán told Jesús. "Evil is everywhere. So is good, but in much smaller doses. I used to think it was a balance, like a scale, you know. Like the rain and sun—as much of one as the other. But now I don't. There is much good, but maybe more evil. That river changed me," he said. "It changed me forever."

"But now you see only evil, Germán," Jesús told him. "Everywhere you look you see only evil. Return to God. You will begin to see clear again. I know your eyes have been sad since then."

And I could see it there too. In the kernel of Germán's black eyes and in the saggy flesh above his eyelids was a long swoop of sadness. Somewhere beyond those opaque eyes was Life, and one time perhaps joy. Joy in La Purísima when he was a boy, a barefoot toddler prancing about, free and unconscious of the world and happily ignorant of the crossing that would come so many years later. His generation's rite of passage was so different from his father's and grandfather's. Before, young men did not typically make the journey. It was true that some did, but it was not a necessity. It wasn't a matter of survival. A man escaped then from a lost love or from the law. It was different then. A man could provide for his family by caring for a small plot of land. It may not have been his own, but he could work it and bring it to its full potential. And once in a while he could take the bus to Villa Madero or Morelia for a movie or a popsicle in the plaza on Sunday. And hold hands with his lover and stroll around the cathedral and look at the things for sale along the porticos.

Jesús' father had told him how you could get your picture taken in front of the cathedral in Morelia for five pesos. Jesús recalled a picture of his mother and father standing together with the cathedral of Morelia in the background.

"There was pride in their eyes," Jesús said. Then he paused. "Well," he said nostalgically. "But it's different now. We cannot make a life there, not now. That's why we will make a life here, *maestro*. We have a chance, you see. Ah, *mi* Dulce," he sighed.

He showed me her picture. She was short, a little stout, dark, and had a perfectly round face. Jesús sometimes called her *mi cuadrito,* my little square, because she was nearly as wide as she was tall. Dulce's complexion was ruddy, but there was an innocent, unknowing beauty in her face. Her name meant sweet, the same term for candy. Dulce and their sons would be leaving soon and would be in Michigan in the next few weeks.

Germán didn't offer to show a picture of Hortencia, so I asked him. Without hesitation he reached into his back pocket and found a leather wallet. Inside was a picture of the two of them seated on a stone bench, flanked by a large, sunlit lake.

"It's in Pátzcuaro," he said. "The lake of Pátzcuaro." Hortencia was younger than Germán. "Seven years," he told me.

"She's pretty," I said. Her hair was straight and as black as onyx. Her eyes too looked like stone and she had long eyelashes that drew you to her like something gentle and sincere, like two waving Japanese fans. Her lips were full, clay colored, and her face was slender and her skin the color of umber. She had a less indigenous look than Dulce. Germán, I knew was twenty-eight, the same age as me. That would make Hortencia only twenty-one.

I wondered how any of the men's belongings, especially pictures had survived the arduous journey and the crossing. With the desert, the water, and the constant threat from *la migra*, it seemed impossible.

"How did these pictures survive the crossing?" I asked.

"We put them in plastic. At the border there are little businesses, selling food, plastic bags, anything you can think of to aid the crossing. For survival people will do what they have to. We put our wallets in a plastic bag and then wrapped it with more plastic. We tied it around our waists and crossed. Other than the clothes on our back, it was all we had," Jesús said.

"But what does a man need?" Germán asked.

I offered the most fundamental response. "Food, water, and warmth, for sure."

"And God," Jesús added. "A man needs God."

"I don't see the use," Germán snapped back. No one spoke for a few moments.

"What about Jennifer?" Jesús asked. I showed the picture that I carried with me. It was a professional photo taken for her college graduation. They thought she looked athletic. I told them she had been a first-rate swimmer for Northwestern. It meant nothing to them.

* * *

Back in Chicago the heat that normally strikes in late August, the dog days of summer, came early. It was June and there had been a succession of steamy days and the beaches were full along the Lake Michigan shore. Jennifer spent the day at North Beach, sunning and playing volleyball. She was a fierce competitor and hated to lose. She hated to lose more than anything.

That day I visited an Egyptian artifact exhibit at the Field Museum. Afterward I went over to the lakefront for the breeze and the generous sunshine. The sailboats were in abundance. Many of them docked here in Burnham Park Harbor and then sailed north along the Michigan side up to Grand Traverse Bay or all the way to Mackinac Island. The sky was clear, but off in the distance, at the horizon, was a thick haze. The heat and the humidity created a gray blanket across the lake.

Jennifer had tickets for the Cubs' game that evening. I planned to meet her at her apartment in Wrigleyville beforehand and from there we would walk to the game. Before that, I was to meet with Professor Lassene to provide a progress report on the dissertation. He and his wife lived near the university in a historic home on 57th Street. I knew his wife Dolores quite well and she hugged me when I entered.

"He's waiting for you," she said through her golden smile. "He thinks so highly of you, Paul. It's finally becoming a reality to him now. He no longer denies it. The finality of his work and the last dissertation is now sinking in."

"I'm grateful," I said respectfully. "I wouldn't want anyone else to guide me on this project. He is the master."

Professor Lassene was a world-renowned anthropologist. His name was familiar in academic circles all over the world. He was widely published and had written several important articles on Rwanda as well as the entire sub-Saharan region. He was best known for a book he wrote on the tribal histories and conflicts in Rwanda. I remember during the 1994 genocide in that country, it was Professor Lassene who the newspapers, magazines, and radio stations consulted on the crisis. I recall listening to him interviewed on NPR providing his expert opinion. And what most amazed me was the objectivity in his analysis. Despite the atrocities he never forgot his role as the observer. He never crossed the line that often appeared so gray to me.

As we talked, he again urged me to travel to Mexico. "The impact on the community there is significant," he told me. But that wasn't my focus.

When the professor spoke his gray eyes burned. They became keen and intense, though outwardly he remained subdued without visible energy. His was a fiery energy that burned inward, like an internal flame. The topic of the dissertation and goal was to address the cherry industry, the workers, output, and assimilation. I still wasn't convinced that a trip to Mexico would be worthwhile for my thesis. Professor Lassene disagreed, but didn't press or require it. I could feel the fading intensity in the professor like a faint, smoldering coal. When he was young it must have burned hotter, like an inferno in search of knowledge. And each time he told me or encouraged me to go to Mexico, I felt it was more for him than for me. It was perhaps his last chance for research. Through me he could once again get his hands dirty, to do what he truly loved and had a passion for.

I looked into his eyes—the same ones that had once swept the plains of Africa and had recorded a permanent picture in his mind. His office at home, like on campus, had an ancient African motif. There were long-faced wooden masks, stretched animal skins, and dark, heavy colors in rugs and paintings. The professor wore a gray cardigan sweater. He laced his fingers together behind his head, crossed his legs, and circled his slippered foot in the pseudo African air. The air was an imitation of that still and dense African air. At our feet were the grassy plains, the rugs, the pictures on the walls were of the Hutu and Tutsi people, and the ceiling was painted the color of a sky somewhere. It was blue with purplish tints and splashes of pink and orange. It was the horizontal sky of Africa, the thing that stretched across the plain in the distance, and the fire that rested on the eternal golden plains.

"The sunset in Africa is endless," he had told me. "At sunset, the horizon burns infinitely. And during the day — heat. The burning heat," the professor would say, reminiscently. "You couldn't escape its reach. Thankfully there is life at the lake. There is survival on the banks of Lake Kivu."

He would talk like this in a rambling stream of consciousness.

"That place along the lake with beautiful interior beaches and dense hills –the land of a thousand hills. And the terrace farming. Karasimbi Volcano aching, trembling the plains at its feet. Now the rivers of Rwanda are again red with blood and scattered with limbs."

He urged me again to see the town, La Purísima. He wouldn't let it go. Perhaps he knew something, or sensed a mysterious call or beckoning. He was a wise man and one much closer to the end than I.

"One of the men didn't make the crossing," I told him. "A group of four men began, but only two crossed. The third man drowned and the final man, the brother of the third, disappeared into the Mexican desert." I paused. "That fourth man's name was Martín. That name, that man haunts me now," I confessed. "His fate and survival consume me now, professor. I don't know why."

He answered wisely. "You are human. There is no shame in that. Okay, you are American, there is a little shame in that," he grinned. He assumed an innocent air of superiority in his French Canadian heritage. "No offense," he assured me.

"None taken."

He reminisced of his time in Africa.

"I had medications and antibiotics for dengue and malaria. The people thought of me as a medicine man," he told me. "I wore a beard and glasses. I could never explain. In the end there is no medicine. There was no medicine for the genocide." He grew serious now. He looked off into the shadows of the room. "There is no medicine for any of us."

"No medicine for the soul," I added.

"I wasn't authorized to administer medicines to the locals, but I did. And once I saved a woman," he told me. "Funny thing, despite the medication, I contracted malaria." He chuckled from the irony. "It's a disease that never leaves you. It lies dormant for a long time, but can ignite again suddenly. It causes fever and horrible sweats. A man can never completely escape it. It struck me again about five years ago. I hope it's the last gasp of the disease. Something worse will take me before it comes again. I'm sure of it."

Dolores came into the study with tea for the three of us. Dolores had taught primary school in the Chicago public schools for over thirty years. She had heard all of his stories and anecdotes many times, but never complained. Somehow I couldn't see Jennifer tolerating it so well. The couple seemed happy. Yet I couldn't help but wonder to myself because in class the professor would speak of marriage rather callously. Institutionalized mating, he called it. "It's the same for every society. By definition, a man made institution." He said it without fail. When I thought of Jennifer again, I realized I was late for the game.

Jennifer and I had met two years earlier at a wedding of a mutual friend. She was full of energy, almost tenacious in all she did. It has always surprised me a little how she would be attracted to me. After all, I was studious, thoughtful, and genuinely scholarly, in short a world-class bore. Those traits seemed to be the things she most detested. But when we began dating she became engrossed with my stories of field studies in Peru and Mexico. Though somehow she thought of those things in the past tense, as if they would not be part of my future, somehow denying in her own mind that my life's work would include much more of it. Of course I insisted that it was a reality, but Jennifer had a vision of the professor, retired to the comforts of his office, like some omnipotent being. She had an ivory tower kind of vision – not exactly reality. Despite all of that, I grew to love her. Her warmth, her wit and smarts, and maybe most her energy. I admired her as much as I loved her. She had earned an MBA from Northwestern and went directly into advertising after graduation. She loved her work. I asked her to marry me after a year of dating. It seemed natural, and truly, I wanted it.

Compiling statistics and data gathering consumed me for the next days. I stared at the raw data from every angle and ran a series of regression models to identify trends. The number of immigrants, the output of the harvests, and the weather conditions were all analyzed and studied clinically and objectively. The men's lives in Michigan were analyzed – the working conditions, the pay, the social networks, the social hierarchy, the political structure, and the pecking order. I reviewed the entirety of my notes and analyzed and compiled. I listened to my cassette recordings again to make sure I hadn't overlooked anything.

Despite all the efforts the thought of Martín lingered in my mind. The thought of a ghost, an angry one, existing in La Purísima, harboring malevolence, floating through narrow dirt streets, and stone homes, casting evil amongst the town, hovered in my head. Or else Martín lived in shame in the mountains and survived as an ostracized leper in the jagged slopes and rocks surrounding the town, never able to return to the town of his birth.

There was no denying that during my study I had grown close to many of the men. Germán and Jesús especially, but others too who had shared stories and family histories. Each of them had a constant theme and it was a longing for La Purísima and familiarity – *tamales pozole, menudo,* and the open, the still air of Mexico, and the mountains, foreboding in the distance. A pace, not slow, but methodic and careless, almost boredom, but something else. Something ancient passed from generation to generation—knowledge of the land and a fear of the gods, superstition, the importance of tradition, and the rite of passage. Today the passage was a geographic transcendence, a dangerous and risky crossing of borders. The passage was a journey into the land of the North, so precise and modern that it paid homage to nothing. It respected neither tradition nor ancestry, simply the god of advancement and accumulation – the new god of the gringos, the god of technology and improvement, and speed and efficiency. The world was fast in the North.

"What's the rush?" one of the men had asked me.

"And then what?" Germán said, throwing his hands up in dismissal. "I care, but maybe not enough. Maybe not as much as people do here. We come out of necessity. We don't come for your culture or history, because to us you have neither."

V

In the Michigan orchards I had grown fond of several of the men and many looked to me for camaraderie or perhaps friendship. But our lives were very different. Many of the men were somber and nothing broke through that shell of bravado. Yet that shell was transparent and nothing but fear lurked beneath it.

Over the past months I had made the trip from Chicago to northern Michigan many times. This time I was not here for work but for solidarity and the sense of ease I found in the company of these men. Gathered, each in our own thoughts and haunted by our own demons, but alive in our own way. I had been accepted by many, while from others I was the eternal outsider, and still others the eternal enemy.

The orchard was unusually cool. The sky was consumed with gray clouds and an intermittent wind stirred, sudden then lazy. The endless churn of the harvest continued, mechanical, men working and picking, and the cycle went on. Many of the men would move on to other orchards after this. Some went to other orchards in Michigan and others went to Ohio or further east. All through the autumn there was always another harvest.

The men had a break in the late afternoon. Germán and Jesús sat with me under a tree and we talked and lifted our faces when the cool, almost damp breeze came. The air was dense with the scent of ripe cherries.

"Any day now they are coming," Jesús reminded us. "Dulce and my two boys. A coyote from Sinaloa will get them across. He knows the border, the tunnels, and where the dangers are. Maybe in a week we will see them." Germán was pensive.

"Maybe we should have used a coyote when we crossed last year," Germán said. "Benito may still be alive," he speculated. "But who knows. We will never know."

"Only God knows," Jesús said. "That is enough."

"Not for me," Germán said. "I wish to know too. Why does *He* have the right? Martín too has the right. If he's alive I'm sure he would like to know." Germán went along with his musings.

Jesús would soon start the factory job and the apartment was ready. He had signed a lease with help from the foreman at the factory.

"Very soon I begin a new life. I tell you, *maestro*, we will never look back."

I allowed the men to talk and rarely inserted my opinion. That is what I had been taught. When asked directly I would delicately skirt the question as if indifferent or just unsure. "Otherwise, you run the risk of destroying the social fabric and natural interaction. You may influence the thinking and opinions of others,"

Professor Lassene had said. "And then, you are not practicing good science."

Later that evening I returned to the familiar hotel along the main street. The harvest was in high gear. The men who didn't go on to other orchards would return to Michoacán and to their wives, children, and families. Germán planned to move on to other harvests and finish with pumpkins in the fall. Jesús would remain. For me, there was a looming sense of closure. My work was approaching its end and there was no reason to return here. The men would soon scatter to other places like nomadic insects. But I still felt that it wasn't complete, as if something was left untied or unfinished. I couldn't name it, but as I lay in bed that night what washed over me was a sense of unfinished business.

It took a long time to fall asleep and I thrashed about in the meantime. Eventually, I must have given in and slept because I woke to the phone ringing sometime in the night. My hand searched and stumbled for the receiver. It was the front desk.

"Sir, I'm so sorry to wake you at this hour," the man's voice said. "But there is a man here who insists on speaking with you. He says it's an emergency."

Without thinking I asked for the time.

"One-thirty," he replied. "The man's name is Germán." He pronounced it funny.

"Send him up."

After flipping on the lamp I slid into a pair of jeans that were hanging over the desk chair. I rubbed my eyelids, heavy and swollen from sleep. I couldn't imagine what it was, but thought something must have happened to one of the men. Perhaps there was an accident or a fight at the orchard. It wasn't uncommon. There was a light tap on the door. I opened it and saw Germán in the shadowy doorway. He looked ghostly and pale, like an old bone. His body was limp and at first he didn't speak. He looked like he could collapse at any moment and the bag he had slung over his shoulder might topple him. I hurried him into the room. He sat in the desk chair beside the crumpled bed.

"What's happened?" I asked.

"It's Hortencia," he said. "She's hurt. Attacked." He spoke the words slowly, without inflection or emotion. It sounded as if he were reading them. Something awful was in his face.

"Attacked?" I asked quietly. My throat had gone dry.

"A man. A man in the night," is all he could say, all he could utter, obviously inebriated by shock.

"How bad?" I asked.

"Bad."

"Do you need to go home?" Germán nodded.

He began to speak, "*maestro*, will you...?" He didn't finish, he was struck too deeply and there was a trailing sense of pathos in his fading, unfinished words. I anticipated his question.

"Go with you?" I asked, finishing what he started. Was I crossing the line? Again he nodded his head. Now his eyes looked helpless and unknowing. He looked as if the blood and energy had drained from his body and all strength had abandoned him. I would go with him.

There was a paralyzing weight in the air. The night went still and a deeper, denser black took it over. It grew quiet and Germán's eyes were now tinged with a far away fear. A dull, somnambulant look had hold of him, as if morphine ran through his veins and sedated him with his own body's protective injection.

"In the morning we'll go to Chicago," I told him.

I offered Germán the bed. At first he resisted, not wishing to put me out. Eventually he crawled on top of the blanket, moving sluggishly like he himself was injured. I'm sure he winced as he laid his head back, his body burdened with the pain of sympathy. I took one of the bed's pillows and used it as a backrest on the desk chair. I settled in, leaving the lamp on. It burned beside me and lit Germán's face. He was stretched out on the bed, looking dead. I could feel my own heart thumping inside my chest, like a quick and persistent hammering. I would go to Michoacán after all. Despite my denial and despite the fact I had found it unnecessary, I was going. Professor Lassene would approve. Jennifer would not.

I struggled to get back to sleep. Something disturbing was in the air. A foul odor or evil aura, a faint, swirling air like from a mound of rotting fruit, a gust of stale ancient air wafting into my head. Or was it only a dream, a memento that lingered in my subconscious from a dream interrupted, dizzying me, my dream cut short by the phone's sharp ring in the dead of night?

The only sound now was the light breathing of Germán. He was asleep. He was orange in the lamp's strange glow and his shadow was tossed on the yellow wall beside the bed. His charcoal skin glowed, almost on fire. He must have dreamed; his eyelids batted violently and he winced from time to time. His gentle, masculine face transformed into one filled with fear. In my head was the odor, the foul thing and with it the thumping of my heart. I switched off the lamp and soon we both slept. The night went quickly.

In the morning Germán woke early. "*Maestro*," he whispered as he lightly wriggled my shoulder, waking me gently. My neck had stiffened during the night. I climbed from the chair. We gathered our things and left the hotel. Germán had a small canvas duffel bag that contained everything he owned here. His whole life in Michigan could be reduced to a small bag. "What else did a man need?" I remembered him asking.

I asked him if Jesús knew what had happened.

"He knows," Germán said. "I told him last night before leaving."

"How did you learn about the attack on Hortencia?"

"A phone call from her sister. We share a phone at the orchard. All of the men have access to it. The call came about eight o'clock last night. The attack happened the night before. I debated coming here. I wasn't sure," Germán admitted.

"I'm glad you did," I assured him.

"Jesús asked me to look for Dulce and the *machitos* when we arrive in La Purísima. They may have already left for the North, but he's worried after hearing of the attack. He's convinced that it's a curse. He told me he would pray for Hortencia and for all of us."

The drive back to the city was quiet. We talked little and stopped only once to eat. Hortencia was in a hospital in Morelia, the capital city of the state of Michoacán. Germán didn't know all the details, but knew that a man had attacked her in her home. He had crawled through a window during the night while she slept.

"She had not been raped, her sister told me. I'm sure

she defended herself," Germán repeated. "I'm sure of it." He refused to think otherwise.

Her condition was serious. She was treated for multiple bruises, lacerations, and a broken arm. From what Germán understood she remained unconscious. But the question of who had done this and why ran through my mind. The only men who remained in town were elderly, not young and virile men motivated to crawl through a bedroom window in the night to assault a young woman.

Germán was quiet, lost in his own thoughts and worry. I wondered what was happening behind those black eyes, in the marrow of his mind. He surely thought, as I did, about who could have done this. And he surely felt anger, a wild spray of anger directed at no one, just a shadow of a man – a sketch of a stranger. Then I thought of what might come next, toppling over the anger, heavier, and stronger—revenge.

We arrived at my apartment in the early afternoon. Immediately I called the airlines to get a flight to Morelia. The evening flight was full so we would have to wait until the following morning. I booked two seats for the flight. My apartment had two bedrooms, one I used as an office and it had a sofa bed. I showed the room to Germán and he dropped his things.

"You have been to Mexico," he said. He pointed his finger to a bookshelf and a picture of me with two Zapotec Indians. "And the *bule,*" he said. There was a large gourd called a *bule* hanging with twine from a nail on the side of the bookshelf. The gourd was dried and gutted, the tip cut off to use as a water canteen by field workers.

"Oaxaca," I told him.

He nodded and a faint smile came across his face.

"But never to Michoacán?" he asked.

"Never."

"Now you will see it, *maestro*."

Until then it hadn't occurred to me that Germán might not have papers. He may not be allowed into his own country. I didn't know if he ever had crossed borders without a cloud of secrecy.

"Do you have documents?" I asked. "To get into Mexico?"

"Yes," he started. "I have a *matrícula*. A kind of passport. Well, it's false, but it will allow me in. I used it when I returned to Mexico a year ago."

I made a call to Professor Lassene and let him know I would be traveling to Mexico. Although the circumstances were precarious, he was pleased that I was going.

"You will complete what you need to for the dissertation—the effects on the town. Remain the observer," he reminded me. "The scientist." I promised and said I would see him when I returned. The professor sounded like he had a cold. "It's the malaria," he told me. "It's acting up again." He left me with that thought.

Whenever I prepared for travel I felt a sense of finality. It was a strange feeling, like I would never return. I felt it a little then as I hung up the phone with Professor Lassene. It was some kind of primal fatalism, I suppose. It made me a little dazed and an unexplainable lethargy would come.

Germán was sitting on the sofa in the front room. Anxiety was in his face.

"Would you like to listen to music?" I asked him. He said he would and I directed him to the stack of CDs next to the stereo. He began sifting through the eclectic collection.

"Who is Billy Bragg?" he asked.

"My hero," I replied. "He sings social ballads, something like socialism."

"Sometimes I think we need that more than God," he said.

I agreed. "Let's listen." He handed me one of the discs, I had them all, and I put it in on the stereo. I excused myself to the other room to call Jennifer. She was at her office. We spoke and agreed to meet for lunch. I had something to tell her.

"And I may have a friend with me," I told her. I hung up the phone and returned to Germán.

"Join us for lunch. I'm meeting Jennifer."

"No, *maestro*," he said, rather insistently. "I'll stay here. I don't feel much like going out. I'm only thinking of Hortencia now. Besides, I'll stay here and listen to your hero."

Back at the orchard men worked steadily, anxious now to finish the harvest. Jesús prayed incessantly, his thoughts consumed with what evil might be settling over La Purísima. He prayed hard that Dulce and the boys would safely escape the town before more violence would strike. He felt relieved that his home was outside of the town itself. He had described the house to me. It was a cement block home with a tin roof. A roof was often a sign of status. Many of the tiny homes had nothing but a dirt floor and the roof was a simple tarp tied down with rope over the dwelling. They would flap like crazy in a strong wind, so must be well tied down. Others, like his, had a tin roof. It was hotter, but provided better protection, yet during strong rains the noise inside was deafening. Other homes still had *teja* roofs, red clay curved tiles. These were of higher status and preferable to the others. As Jesús proudly told me, his home had the largest and most beautiful bougainvillea in the area.

"It's deep pink," he said. "Most admired, and such a sight against the dull wall of my home."

And behind the tiny home was a small, but fertile plot of land. In the distance was the sierra—the forbidding Sierra de Mil Cumbres. Jesús' sister and her husband would occupy his home for as long as he was in Michigan. They would care for the home, tend to the field, the calves, and to the two dogs.

"And the horse," Jesús told me. "He's not much, *maestro*. Poor thing, the beast's ribs show. He spends his days tied to a eucalyptus tree out front. I don't know what makes him work, but he pulls the plow with me behind. Tilling... tilling... It's a kind of energy that comes from deep in the animal's spirit. And the boys run barefoot," he reminisced. "They race along the grassy edges of the field. The grass and mud underneath is cool." He quickly returned to the present. "But as I've told you, that's not the life for them. I want them to prosper and with God's help they will. In Mexico we plant seed by hand. Days are spent hunched over like an old man with a curved spine, digging, dropping seed, and covering it again with soil. It isn't like here. No modern machines to turn the soil or plant seed. Harvest is by hand, not by some insect-like machine with metal arms and cogs and turning parts. No, it's simple there, *maestro*. But difficult, too difficult," he said and then he shook his head to negate the place and the land that seemed too hard for him.

The Michigan harvest would complete soon. I imagined the orchard with its trees bent in stride like a leaning, distorted man aged by years of work in the fields. The sky would be swift and long feathery clouds would sweep across the deep blue Michigan sky. The clouds came off the lake from Canada, dense sometimes, filled with moisture. And they dropped their payload, gentle at times, other times relentless on the rolling, green Michigan landscape.

I left the apartment and walked a long way before catching a cab. I liked to walk alone. In the city I would promenade the streets surrounding the university and around Hyde Park, or visit cafés and sit sometimes until closing in an unfamiliar place. I would sit at a corner table or a small one pushed against a dark wall, avoiding tables near a window along the street. At these places I would read novels and venture out in spirit along the story's path of silk or rugged landscape. It didn't matter. And the next time I would find another less familiar locale with busy streets where a café, perhaps in Pilsen, nestled between restaurants or bakeries. To me, it was of no consequence. If I found a café that I most liked I would eventually return, but not too soon. An adequate period of absence would lie between visits so that no place would become familiar. I think familiarity was the thing I disliked most. Or was it true that I was such a slave to routine and conformity and this great conscious effort to scout out new places to frequent was my desperate attempt to escape my own lack of nouveau? I suppose it didn't matter. We all behave in ways for different reasons—some conscious, most just a reflection of our own neuroses. It may have been just a game to escape myself. Still, I enjoyed my strolls and visits to cafés throughout the city, hidden behind the pages of a Thomas Wolfe or Malcolm Lowry novel, sipping a black coffee. I was seldom, if ever, recognized and I found that strange unfamiliar nuance so appealing that I sought it out, like a narcotic, whenever I could. What urged me along was simply the possibility of being cradled in the arms of unfamiliarity and to be recognized merely as a calm, quiet stranger.

And then I met Jennifer. My walks became shorter; the cafés were closer to home and more recognizable. More often people noticed me, and the coffee tasted the same —common and trendy. It had lost that taste of foreignness and the earthy, almost smoky quality I had grown to love and somehow gave me an injection of Life. My life's radius enclosed. I became swallowed by my own desire or need to see Jennifer. Despite her less than enthusiastic interest in the merits of anthropological science, I loved her. Her skin had such a clean, shiny quality, almost like it was too small for her frame. The skin stretched to get around her broad swimmer's shoulders, shiny from the effort.

I can think now of her body, hard and beautiful, glowing in the dim light of my apartment. In the corner of my room are the floating green eyes of the black onyx jaguar that I had brought from Oaxaca. Jennifer's body and the jaguar's eyes are mystic and somehow it seems they belong together. One transposed onto the other— the sexless jaguar and Jennifer—its eyes and her body. Many times our bodies entwined in the dark night, I stared, almost hypnotic into the fierce eyes of the jaguar—the totem of pre-Hispania, the first ancestor of Mexico. The animal most feared and admired by the Olmec, the mother culture of Mexico. The eyes frightened Jennifer. Many times she asked me to cover them before we slept. I coldly refused, oddly finding comfort in that glow, those deep green marbles in the night, watching our bodies wound together in love and in sleep. I denied Jennifer a sound sleep as she sensed her body keenly watched through the night.

Jennifer met me for lunch at a restaurant in the financial district.

"Where's your friend?" she asked right away.

"At the apartment."

"Alone?" she asked, full of surprise.

"He is."

"Is this friend from the university?"

"No, he's one of the men from the Michigan orchards." I shocked her.

"Are you doing charity work now?" she asked sarcastically. "And you trust him alone in your apartment?"

"Of course. That's what I wanted to tell you, Jen. I'm going to Mexico with him. There's been an accident or something and his girlfriend is in the hospital. I don't know all the details." Jennifer had a look of confusion. She grew serious.

"And what can you do?" she asked.

"He asked me to go with him and the truth is I want to go. I should be gone no longer than a week."

"But we have the fittings for the bridesmaids' dresses this weekend," she stuttered, stumbling for an excuse. "Lauren and Courtney will be in town. I wanted us all to get together afterward." She went on. "Paul..."

"Look, I'm sorry," I said calmly. "I just won't make it. You won't even know I'm missing, Jen. You'll be so absorbed with colors, ribbons, and shoes. The fashion."

"Perhaps," she gave in. "Only a week?" she asked.

"No more."

The following week Jennifer was traveling for work—to New York for a new client. Her career was so important to her and demanding, she'd hardly know I was away.

When I returned to the apartment I found Germán asleep on the sofa. He was sitting; his head shot back with the music playing. For a moment I stood watching him rest and then walked into my bedroom. The voice of rebelliousness and tenderness sang on. The voice delivered simple lyrics that rounded the corner and seeped into my room...

From the Land of the Midnight Sunglasses
To the Mountains of the Moon
You could never stay a day too long
Nor never come back too soon.

The words gently filled the room, engulfing me with emptiness. I felt a raw sense of fatalism wash over me, like something hollow and vacant. The black onyx jaguar, with his sharp eyes, didn't watch me now, his eyes not at all spectacular in the daylight. They were dull and opaque by day, asleep, born only in the unfathomable night. Eyes like the nocturnal burst of a flower that blooms only in the black of night and cowers within itself by day.

And you know what a fool I am
With my short attention span
Flying in the rainy season too,
Nothing can keep me away from you

I slowly gathered my things for the trip, stopping at times as a rush passed through me. It would linger in my abdomen, circle like an eagle searching for a perch, until it hollowed me, and then sail off with weightless wings. I would start again until the bird would return to circle the hollow, the vacant space that paralyzed me.

As I packed the thought of the missing man returned. Martín seemed to share the space with me; his story and his destiny now consumed me. I wondered then if Martín knew a god, if he looked to the sky, earth, or ocean for redemption and for salvation. Germán had turned away from his God, a God that he saw now as malevolent—an angry force capable of evil.

Jesús was forever faithful. He turned more to his God now, and the saints and virgins that he knew could grant miracles. He bowed to them and spoke their names...*La Virgen de Guadalupe, La Virgen de la Salud,* ... lit candles and kneeled before the hopeful flicker. He prayed for Hortencia's recovery and for his dream of a life in the North and for the safe passage of his family. He was a man alone with a dream, and he did the same as many strong, but simple men of the world do. I finished packing. In the morning we would leave for Mexico.

VI

We arrived at O'Hare Airport in plenty of time before the flight, but already there was a twisting line of people waiting to check in. The counters hadn't opened and people were anxious, huddled with loads of baggage, bulging boxes held shut with twine, and children in tow. There were men with serious eyes and women with the look of long suffering on their faces. It had been over a year since my last trip to Mexico. I most remembered the children from Oaxaca: the little black heads, full and thick like suede. Small children scurried under the ropes that held a queue of people together, playing tag and laughing. I watched them the most. In front of me was a young woman with a toddler clinging to her bare leg. His eyes were glued to mine. I smiled at his bewildered face. He stared back like a stone.

Eventually the line began to crawl; we checked in and boarded. As we ascended, I watched the Chicago skyline disappear in the morning haze. The last thing I saw was the Ferris wheel at Navy Pier. It drew my eyes, motionless in the morning hour, waiting to circle tourists all day for a view of the city's skyline and the lake. Germán sat beside me leafing through a magazine.

"I need to find out who did this to Hortencia," he said.

"But first," I said, "see to it that she's well." He agreed. Any thoughts of revenge would wait until Hortencia was recovered, or at least until she was well enough to return to La Purísima.

The town had no hospital so she mended in Morelia. Germán believed she would recover. Hortencia's sister had been optimistic.

"But *maestro*, I'm more concerned about after she is well. I mean, after her body is healed."

"Why is that?"

"I'm worried about her mind," he answered. "How will her mind be? All full of fear? Will she hide in the shadows afraid to leave her own home? Of course, even there she may feel fear. That's where the attack happened." He went on with much anxiety in his voice, concerned that he would suffer for another man's actions.

"We can only wait, I suppose," are the words I offered him. "Once she is home we will see."

"I fear she will push me away," he said before drifting his attention to the empty sky. He sharply turned topics. "Well," he began, "you will see how we live, *maestro*. My parents' home is small and simple. You will see," he told me, making sure my expectations were sufficiently low.

Germán had a friend living in Morelia, where he would stay until Hortencia was released from the hospital. I preferred a hotel and would find a room in the city. Once Hortencia was well enough we would travel together to La Purísima.

"And we'll visit the lake," Germán insisted. "The famous Lake Pátzcuaro. It's no more than an hour bus ride from Morelia. I will show you, *maestro*," he said, as if caring for me.

Germán sat beside me with a calming, central force. It was something like grace I thought. His black, watery eyes would look at me with indifference, like he cared for nothing. Yet I sensed urgency inside him and a burning need to know what had happened to Hortencia. His exterior remained calm and graceful, but underneath the facade of stoicism was urgency. Beyond the stone eyes and somber looks was an anxious man who at times seemed uncomfortable in his own dark skin. To know! He must have thought. He surely anticipated sitting beside Hortencia's bedside where he would comb her black hair and stroke her naked, bronzed arms. And maybe whisper a ballad in her ear, one of love and one of a lover's return. Of longing – a song of lovers separated by the cruelty of economics, the ancient hymn of disparity that played softly and eternally in the heads of lovers all over the world.

Sometimes the world is unfair. That didn't matter now. He must know. And perhaps in the back of his mind a suspicion lurked. In the shallow margins of his mind, a suspicion so impossible, yet it could not be ignored. It had been over a year. Most thought he was dead. Martín. Wasn't he dead, just a skeleton in the Coahuilan desert? Was he nothing more than vacant eyes and bare ribs, just a decoration for the Day of the Dead? He thought of the man that said Martín was just an angry ghost. Ice ran through Germán's veins – a cold, intangible fear of ghosts, of something beyond this life and its struggle. His poverty was not a crime. It was nobody's crime, just cruel—most of all it was cruel.

* * *

The town's name, La Purísima, meant purity. Once benign and colorless, it now suspected and feared one of its own. It remained virtually unchanged since the beginning of the last century. La Purísima hadn't seen violence since the revolutionary period of the 1920s, and even then it was infrequent. As the plane descended it was obvious how green and fertile the landscape was surrounding the city of Morelia. What struck me was how the green hugged the earth like a well-made carpet.

"It's been raining," Germán said as he leaned and gazed out the plane's window. "This land is so fertile," he said thoughtfully. "It's perfect for agriculture. But we are entitled to so little that we can't earn a living."

From the air the rolling landscape sprawling away from the city was lush and dark. Bright greens cascaded toward the city and the nearby mountains were dense with trees. We could clearly see the epicenter of the city; it was the cathedral. Every Mexican city and town has a church and it is the focal point and heart of the city. Everything else builds around it. In Morelia, it was a two-towered edifice. Two spires pierced the sky like cone-shaped spacecraft. All else drew toward it, or pulled away depending upon one's opinion of the church.

We took a taxi into the city. The car drove alongside the retired aqueduct that divided the avenue. We peered under the arches at cars leaving the city. Along the avenue were tidy plazas and old stucco homes with lazy verandas that had been converted into museums. We approached a *glorieta*, circled, and began towards the downtown.

"It's called Tarascas Fountain, named after the regional Indians," Germán said as we passed the *glorieta* with the impressive fountain in the center. We went along the primary avenue, which was lined with shops, a judicial building, banks, and more. The street was busy and it grew more crowded and thick with packs of people as we drew closer to the city's center.

"The cathedral is ahead," Germán said, pointing his finger. From the front seat of the taxi I leaned forward and dipped my neck to where I could get a glimpse of the church.

"Hospital Morelos," Germán said to the driver. "Do you know it?"

"Of course," the driver replied confidently. "It's very near to here, only five blocks."

He sped up a little. We passed the cathedral on our left and could see it surrounded with vendors peddling clay things, fruits, and other colorful wares. There were narrow one-way side streets flooded with people. A bus roared past our taxi and a blast of gray-black smoke shot up, choking us. A block or two beyond we turned onto a side street that was nearly impassable. Both sides were lined with parked cars and a policeman stood in the center, carelessly waving his hands and intermittently blowing into a whistle.

"Welcome to Mexico, *maestro*," Germán said. The taxi squirmed its way through the labyrinth and we soon gained speed until we reached the hospital. The taxi let us out in front and we both went inside. Germán hurried to the reception desk and I waited behind, fidgeting uncomfortably. Quickly he returned with the room number.

"I shouldn't go," I told him.

"No," he said. "Come along. I've told Hortencia about you." I didn't resist. We found the elevator and were soon on the third floor.

"Room three twelve," he said. Germán walked quickly ahead of me, his head darting from side to side like a pendulum, searching anxiously for the room. "It's here!" he called to me before disappearing into a doorway up ahead. When I reached it, I awkwardly poked my head around.

The room was dark and at first my eyes wouldn't see, blinded by the room's darkness and maybe too by what I feared to see. Then I noticed the window and the blinds pulled half shut. I could see a dark shadow lying in the bed and I recognized Germán leaning over it. It was a narrow and erect mound of bedding, motionless like a stiffly rolled rug. There was another person in the room, a woman I sensed. Hortencia's sister. Germán noticed me.

"Come in, *maestro*. "It's okay," he assured me. His voice more calm than it had been only minutes before; he sounded comforted in some way.

The room smelled heavily of antiseptic and I thought of the thick, heavy air of sickness as I entered. How could anyone endure the sights and scents of illness or injury? My eyes adjusted to the dim light and I met a face, naturally slender, now swollen and bruised. Part of me wanted to shrink and turn back. I remembered the picture Germán had shown me. The face little resembled what I recalled. The eyes were shut by swollen lumps of flesh above the eyes. Her lips were enlarged and there was a bandaged cut on the bottom lip and another, larger bandage stretched across her ash colored forehead.

"Hortencia, this is Paul." Nervously, I eased to the bedside and noticed one of her slender hands along the bed rail. My hand slid down to find a flaccid hand and I squeezed it gently. No words came from my lips, though some simple greeting skipped through my head. Her face changed then. Her swollen cheeks drew up, her eyes became more squinted now, and her lips quivered. It was difficult to find in the distorted face, but it was a smile. Instantly I did the same and I think she acknowledged it. Her sister, a younger and lighter haired girl, sat in the corner with her hands folded. Knitting sat beside her. She had been at Hortencia's bedside since she had arrived. She was quiet and smiled shyly.

Germán leaned over Hortencia and pressed his mouth to her ear and carefully embraced her fragile body. Soon I noticed her eyes growing moist, and a tear slid down the side of her swollen face. I wondered if he whispered loving things, asked of the attack, or quietly sang a ballad of lovers reunited. It didn't matter; he said things that only two lovers know. Things that only Germán and Hortencia shared, their own private poetry.

There was a sense of calm in the room. A quiet, wistful thing, that seemed to rise from the embracing couple. The sister must have sensed it too, but no one spoke. Soon I left the room; I would return tomorrow. I needed to find a hotel room and hoped to find one in the historic district.

After hailing a taxi I was back again near the cathedral and the city's beating heart—its swelling and contracting soul. I felt I knew Mexico, but I knew more of the rural places, the wide-open landscape and the agrarian people. My time in Oaxaca had been spent among the Zapotec Indians. Each region of Mexico is different. Each has a unique culture, cuisine, and sometimes language and dialect, or at least a different rhythm and cadence.

Near the cathedral I found a room at a hotel called La Alameda. The room was on the second floor and had a window overlooking Abasolo. Just below was the top of a forest green awning capping a first floor window. The building was constructed of a gray stone, thick enough to shelter the guests from the noise of the streets. I stayed in the room until it was dark and then went out to find something to eat. The main streets were well lit. The main avenue that ran in front of the cathedral was called Madero. On either side of the avenue were black iron lanterns mounted high along handsome stone walls and buildings. The lanterns put out good light and the avenue looked pretty as I gazed down it, like a stone tunnel lit evenly along the way. Above, the night sky was bright, but there was a looming blackness and uncertainty in a mass of colliding clouds in the distance.

Near the corner of Madero and Abasolo was a restaurant called *La Puerta Verde,* The Green Door. The building had several small balconies, big enough to stand on, with potted plants holding red flowers that looked like geraniums. I went in and found a small shop downstairs selling lithographs and photos of old Morelia. The restaurant was upstairs and I climbed the staircase of wood and iron. It wasn't crowded; there were only a few tables filled with couples and another with a family of four. The setting was rustic and there were many 19th Century photographs of Morelia when it was called Vallolidad. From my table I could see one of the balconies across the room. The wooden shutters leading to it were open and the sounds of the street were rising up.

After ordering I walked to the balcony and stepped out, gripping the simple iron rail surrounding it. To the left was the brightly lit cathedral and surrounding it were the tightly packed vendors. The stands were now converted into food places selling tacos, tamales, and sweet things. A man slapped freshly made tortillas between his hands. Under a blue tarp I could see smoke rising as beef cooked and a single light bulb lit the space. I smelled the meat, the smoke and other scents, dense and sweet. And the night air threatened rain; it smelled of coming moisture.

Directly across from the balcony was a tree-lined plaza and at the end was a stately looking judicial building. Below, people scurried in twos and threes, while others went in swarms along the avenue. Some hurried, but most went limply, in a fashion ignorant of time. People enjoyed a carefree stroll along the downtown streets and went for coffee or for the vendors and the smoky, gritty taste of the street.

As I watched the people I thought of Martín. Had he drifted into this city and become lost in its density, its faceless, nameless mass? I looked off into the distance, but all I could see was black. It was sky and mountain fused into one voluminous mass threatening to swallow the city.

"*Señor*?" a tiny voice came from behind me. "*A comer*," she said. My food was ready. I ate and when I finished it was raining. I hurried back to the hotel. That night it rained heavily and thunder rolled over the city from the black mountains. Lightning flashed and my room glowed like daylight in the middle of the dark Mexican night. The low, black sky moved in and covered the city. Thunder rolled as if the ground itself moved or nearby a volcanic mountain stirred, rumbling and belching ash, erupting the clouds that showered over the city of Morelia.

By early morning the storm had passed. The city woke to clear sky, swatches of blue and full creamy clouds. The damp was diminishing, making room for the approaching heat. The air was fresh, cleaned like the streets and the souls of the city. The rain had washed away the scents from the night before. All that remained was a clean, scentless air. At a restaurant across from the cathedral, I sat in the cool shade of the porticos. Little birds, colorless things, hopped and pecked around the sidewalks, snatching specks of food that the rains had washed in.

"Coffee, *señor*?" the waiter asked. "We have the coffee of Uruapan, if it pleases you." Mexico's best coffees come from Chiapas and Veracruz. There was a region near here, by the city of Uruapan, which also grew coffee. The city was west of here, beyond Lake Pátzcuaro. The waiter returned with sweet breads; I enjoyed the bread with the black, earthy coffee of Uruapan.

At a nearby table I noticed two Americans. A father and son it seemed. Their backs faced me and as they looked at each other to speak I noticed their profiles were identical. Each had a long, straight nose, and a sharp chin, like twins, only thirty or so years apart. The older man, the father, looked comfortable, as if he knew the place well. I wondered what a man did here. If they glanced at me they may have wondered the same.

Soon I was back at the hospital. Germán was there and so was Hortencia's sister, a name I never learned. I told Germán where I was staying.

"She's much better. Don't you think?" he asked me, never taking his eyes off of her.

"She looks much better," I responded sincerely. Hortencia's face was less swollen and more resembled the picture he had shown me. There was evidence of a slender face, smooth, bronze skin, and bright eyes. She spoke in more than a whisper. She didn't recall much of the attack that night. All she remembered was that she woke with a man in her bed, on top of her. She may have struggled in her sleep, for how long she couldn't say.

"The room felt cool. The window where he had entered was open," she said. He was heavy upon her and strong. The stranger smelled different, dank, like the damp earth, like he had crawled from a hole deep within it. "It was a moonless night," she said.

"Did he speak?" Germán asked. Hortencia paused, as if she didn't want to answer or was unable to. She was afraid or ashamed to speak.

"Did he?" Germán asked again more sternly. "Tell me!" For courage, Hortencia turned to her sister.

"Tell him," she said, almost in a whisper. We both turned to Hortencia for the words.

"He said," she began slowly, like she was winding up or avoiding the words.

"Well!" Germán said to her, pulling the words from her.

"What he said is this is for Germán." Germán stared at her and it seemed a thief had snatched his energy. It was gone in one violent motion in those sparse, simple words. In a second, with those words, "this is for Germán," his life went gray. He shrank from the bedside.

Hortencia was turned; her face buried in pillow and gathered bedding. She wept shamefully, her body heaving beneath the sheets. There was only one thought, one thread, and one strange man in my mind. Martín. I saw it in Germán's face, the ghost of the crossing was the only explanation.

"Martín," Germán said quietly, but defiantly. He said it again, "Martín," almost in disbelief and his face was like stone, his black, watery eyes still and fixed, gone missing in thought. For a few moments his spirit left us.

The sister was moved to tears and she hurried to comfort Hortencia. There were inaudible words between them, just whispers through tears. Out of ignorance, or a paralyzing uncertainty, my feet were anchored. As the two women comforted one another, Germán and I stood stately, reserved and separated by much physical space and perhaps more by emotional space. I thought how predictable this circumstance was and common in so many cultures. The women externalize and comfort one another. They weep openly and bare the emotion attempting to heal the wound. Meanwhile, the male internalizes, withdraws into himself, into his own thoughts, and recedes into the darkest recesses of his soul. And for a moment, I understood why the world has seen so much war.

I realized then that I had retreated from the bedside. I was nearer the doorway now, further from the unfolding life before me. We are forever the observers I thought— the clinical, objective men of anthropological science. But then, I sensed an anger come over me, or empathy. I don't know what it was except it drew me again to the bedside. I was pulled to the weeping and inwardly urged to the black eyes of Germán.

"We don't know for sure," I said almost as a reflex to

the silence. "It may not have been Martín." I don't know why I said it—we knew.

"I know," Germán said. "It's Martín and I'll find him. We have to go to La Purísima."

"We will," I said. "But not without Hortencia. She must be well first." Germán turned to me. His will was strong. Germán turned again to the bed where the sisters were embracing. He approached them.

I felt faint. The room's air seemed thin now, insufficient for four. I retreated again and returned to the street where I could breathe more easily. The street was noisy and smelled of exhaust and the new scents of the day; it was singularly sweet and awful. I sat on a nearby step and pushed my hair back, perspiring but breathing again. Cars whistled past, rattling; it was beginning to get hot.

VII

The city was coming alive again and I wondered what moved this place. What made this country get up each morning? I recalled again my time in Oaxaca. I recalled the vacant stares of the people, indifferent or uncaring. It was as if nothing mattered, not even Death. Or was it they were numbed, anesthetized by so much Life, color, suffering and tragedy? Too much history, too much superstition and fear?

A taxi dropped me near the hotel. I didn't enter. The downtown was full of voices, of stands, of horns, and of people. I walked the porticos, curious why vendors were allowed to de-beautify the colonial city. It was a challenge to pass; junk and imitation goods cluttered the path. I crossed Avenue Madero and went near the cathedral. The street was lined with buses and street merchants surrounded the cathedral. Ugly blue and red tarps stretched over their stands for protection from the sun and from the sudden, explosive rains. The rains would come often in the early afternoon or in the late, sleepy time of the day.

A small child, his face smeared with dirt, came to me with a tiny brown hand out for money or to sell little packets of gum. Others waved cheap woven baskets in front of me while searching my face for interest, anything other than the hopelessness that consumed their own eyes. There was a hollow thud up ahead at the corner of the plaza, a constant thud, dull and persistent. A woman, in a white cotton dress, loose and crinkly, covered with a faded apron brought her hand down. Again and again it dropped in a swift, practiced motion. Her long, gray-black hair was pulled back neatly and gathered with a colorful band. She clutched a machete and in a rhythmic, precise manner the machete fell on a coconut. She worked like a machine. Her hand fell again and again. When it split she had coconut milk to sell. Her heavy, dark legs were spread wide for leverage and again the hammer, the persistent thud, and finally the victory. Crack! And the sweet milk.

"Coco!" a man shouted. "Coco...!"

A stray dog trotted awkwardly up ahead. I followed it around toward the center of the plaza. The dog was covered with matted fur and its back torso hung low, nearly dragging on the ground. It was more open here, with scattered stone benches and eucalyptus trees lining the way. People sat and enjoyed the midday sun or shade while pigeons pecked nearby. These were the common people – the lower economic class. I had seen all classes in Mexico and Peru. In both, the lower classes, the most indigenous, were the simplest but possessed the most appeal. They would swarm together in public places with an ancient charm and grace. In both countries the middle and upper classes imitated the United States and Europe. They formed an anti-intellectual force, feigning high culture and interest in art and literature. It was the bourgeoisie as anywhere else in the world. I had thought of them before as classless. Not of strata or rank, but of style and grace. Grace particularly eluded them. And the women, their use of makeup, like gore painted around their eyes and mouths was vulgar. This group repulsed me more than the peon, because the lower class imitated nothing. They were too poor for cheap and badly worn imitations.

It was noontime and I wandered back to the hotel. I had no more than entered my room when the phone rang. The front desk had a visitor.

"Send him up," I instructed the man.

"No, sir, only guests are allowed into the rooms. You will have to come down."

As I was returning to the lobby, I remembered that Germán was the only one that knew I was here. And it was Germán standing now just outside the hotel entrance, looking off into the busy street.

"Come in!" I called to him above the hound of traffic. "It's hot out there in the sun."

"No," he said. "It's fine for me." I walked out onto the sun-drenched sidewalk and to the hum of traffic and the sharp, startling car horns.

"Strange policy," I mused. "They won't allow visitors up."

"I'm not surprised," he said. "Though it's a selective policy." I didn't know what he meant and had a confused look on my face. "The policy is not the same for all men," he said as he pointed to his arm, the charcoal tone, and then to his face, the indigenous features. "Sometimes we are not even accepted in our own country."

"Ignorance," I said.

"Well," he said, "and fear, too I suppose."

"Perhaps," I said.

"We can adopt the names of the Spanish and Mestizo, Juan or Pablo, but we can't change the dark color of our skin or change our features," he said. "The worst treated are the Tarascos. We don't have it so bad."

Germán made excuses for the injustice. Perhaps because it had been so long, so many centuries of persecution. In this matter his will was not as strong, or it had not yet been tested. I felt his powerful will boiling in need to avenge Hortencia's attack. But here he dismissed it, denied it, or burrowed it further inside him. Buried in a place that would some day eat and burn away at his soul and spirit. And like a boll weevil gorging on cotton, it would steal his will and eventually his soul. Injustice will eat a man alive.

"Let's walk," I told him. We started out but it was hot. "There," I pointed to a sidewalk café shaded by an awning. He hesitated, perhaps unsure.

We sat at a table and chairs made of pigskin and palm stalks called *equipales.* There was a canary colored tablecloth with a smaller, blue and red checked one spread across the top. We each ordered a beer with salt and lemon.

"Hortencia will leave the hospital tomorrow," he informed me.

"Good." I smiled. "She's better then."

"It will take several more days rest at home. But she will be well enough tomorrow to return to La Purísima. You will have to stay at my parents' home. There aren't hotels in La Purísima," he said, staring into his beer glass. "No tourists I'm afraid. In fact, I had never stayed at a hotel until that night in Michigan," he admitted without shame.

We both heard a strange bird sound nearby. It was coming from near one of the large clay pots adorning the café corners. The pots contained hibiscus and long wavy grasses. A boy's head popped up. He had sandy hair and both teeth were missing up front.

"Coo! Coo!" he called like a dove, but with a higher pitch. He realized I saw him and he immediately raised an index finger to his lips to hush me. As if to say, "don't give away my position. Don't expose me."

My attention shifted back to the table and I ignored the boy. We ate in the shade of the awning, entertained by the intermittent song of the dove-boy. Afterward Germán was anxious to return to the hospital.

"Meet me tomorrow at the hospital, *maestro*, about noon. That's when Hortencia will be discharged. When we get to La Purísima we begin our search for Martín."

"And when we find him?" I asked.

"I don't know yet," he answered. "Martín has a lot of grief and shame, but it was wrong what he did. Maybe it was wrong to cross the river when and where we did, but he can tell me that. But this was wrong. Nothing will bring his brother back—nothing. Who knows why things happen, *maestro*? They just do. And that's all." Germán hurried off while I stayed behind for another Pacifico. The little dove-boy sounds persisted and the head poked out again.

"*Hola*," I said to him. He leaned from behind the flowers and grasses. He returned the greeting in Spanish and then he said, "I speak English too." And he did, very well.

"Did you see me over there?" he asked, pointing to the large terra cotta pot.

"Of course, and I heard you too."

"Yes, I was making bird sounds."

"I know," I told him. I asked him to sit with me at the table. His name was Claudio and he was eight years old. I told him my name. He was fair skinned with light eyes and his cheeks were full, like round balls when he smiled. His mouth seemed large for his face.

"Are you here alone?" I asked him.

"No, my father is inside the hotel next door for a meeting."

"I see," I said. "What kind of meeting?"

He didn't know, but told me they were all old people. I laughed.

"My father is old," he proceeded to tell me. "He should have twenty or thirty years like you, but he has sixty-one years. Can you believe that?"

I said it was possible. "And your mother?"

"Oh, she is young." I asked him if he lived nearby. He did, here in Morelia.

"Did you learn English in school?" I asked and complimented him on his pronunciation. He smiled and chuckled, the way a child does, but he spoke maturely.

"They don't teach me a thing in school," he said. "I learned English from my father. He is from California. I'm learning French too, but at home instead of school. A lady comes to my house for the lesson. And guess what?"

"What?" I went along.

"No uniforms!" he exclaimed.

"And how about your mother?" I asked.

"She's from Mexico. From a city called Zamora."

"You've got the best of both worlds then," I told him.

"Did you hear me making those bird sounds over there?" he asked again, making sure I hadn't forgotten his special skill.

"Of course I heard you, Claudio."

"My mom calls me *pajarito,* little bird," he told me excitedly and smiled big and his cheeks drew into little balls. His eyes changed into straight lines, like thin shards of glass. He was thinking of his mother. "And you know there is a street near my home called *La Calle de Los Pájaros*? The Street of the Birds. And whenever we drive along that street she tells me that this is the street of my parents. My parents live here." Claudio and I laughed together.

"Your mother likes to tease you," I said. "She sounds nice."

"I have two brothers. Both are probably older than you," he began. "One has thirty-six years and the other has thirty-eight years. Can you believe it?" He looked away as in deep thought. "One has the same name as you, Paul."

"And what will you do when you grow up, Claudio?" I asked. "What will you study?" Looking to the sky, he concentrated intensely.

"I love the planets. Yes," he paused. "Maybe I'll study the planets." He seemed convinced.

"And you?" he asked.

"Well, I'm still studying. Can you believe it?" I asked him jokingly.

"Studying what?"

"Anthropology."

"Ohhhh," he said, in a drawn out very knowing way, nodding his head. But he was only a child after all.

"Do you know what that is?" I asked.

"No." He smiled. I was about to explain when we both noticed a group of men, old and deliberate, exiting the hotel next door. There were eight or ten men gathered.

"It's Joe!" Claudio shouted and ran quickly toward the men. One noticed him running and I heard him say "Claudio", and they slapped their hands together when they met. I watched the group swallow the boy. He became lost and then they were gone.

I walked again and drifted in front of a building that was once a convent, now used as an artisan's showcase. For sale were wooden things, wool clothes, and black lacquer plates from around the state of Michoacán; beside it was an open-air market. Again, there was the light blue canopy secured with twine and underneath were pottery, woven things, baskets, and scents sweet and foul, hats, junk, and more junk. There were shifty, untrusting eyes, blaring radios, children scampering, and a pervading kind of boredom. I thought about Jesús' boys and realized they wouldn't have such advantages as Claudio.

An Indian woman sold colorful cotton smocks with embroidery in front. Her hair was woven into a thick braid and she had three daughters nearby. They had large droopy mouths, pigtails, and played on the steps of the cultural building. They were each under five and wore dirty, thick cotton sweatpants that looked padded. The girls bounced and slid along the steps and the older girl picked up the younger one, who sat with her whole dark fist in her mouth. The mother took no notice, too busy struggling to earn the day's meal.

VIII

The following day Hortencia was discharged from the hospital. A nurse pushed her through the lobby in a wheelchair, flanked by Germán and her sister. Hortencia looked better. Weak and sore but well enough to return home. The four of us went out to the sidewalk where a bus stop was close by. Hortencia leaned on Germán and her sister hung close behind.

"This bus will take us to the central bus station," Germán said. "That's where we can catch a bus for La Purísima. It's a long ride, *maestro*," he warned me.

"It's fine for me," I told him. "My only concern is Hortencia."

We waited over an hour at the bus station. The bus had mechanical problems and it took some time to locate the necessary replacement part and then the time to fix it. There were many eyes upon me and for a time I felt misplaced. I was suddenly a minority. People waited on benches or directly on the cement floor, fanning themselves. They did what people did here; they waited.

Despite the delay, there was no concern, no immediacy from the waiting passengers. And there was even less urgency from the mechanic and the driver. It was just accepted. Things get done when they get done. If not now, then later, and if not later then tomorrow. And then, well, "when God wishes." Besides, what could there possibly be in La Purísima worth rushing for? I supposed little and waited with the rest of them.

We finally struck out onto the road, heading south from the city. As the bus wound around the hilly, two-lane road I looked back to Morelia in the small valley below. The cathedral was the most noticeable landmark. On the near margins of the city were tight rows of tiny apartment houses, stone buildings, each with its own water tank on top. They looked like long rows of little black buffalo.

"All government housing," Germán told me. "But they don't do enough."

Germán and Hortencia sat in the seat in front of me. She rested her head on his shoulder as he did his best to brace her body from each bump and sway. Hortencia's sister sat beside me. The seats were close together and my knees were firmly shoved into the back of Germán's seat. As we drove further from the city, the landscape rolled and became mountainous.

Off to the east were the jagged and remote Sierra de Mil Cumbres. The land, green and dense, was farmed sporadically. There were fallow fields along the slopes and cornfields stretched on the level plain nearer the roadside. The towns we went through or passed near had Indian names like Tiripetío and Atecuaro, while others combined an indigenous language with Spanish, like Acuitzio del Canja. Cattle grazed at the foot of the black mountains on the horizon. Light and shadow swept across them, for a moment green and then suddenly black. On the mountain slopes were cloud forms, shadows born from the clouded mirror above. The bus was full of women, children, old men, and a caged chicken. A woman sang quietly, somewhere in the multitude behind us.

It grew hot. The windows would only come part way down. We reached Villa Madero.

"It's called the crossroads," Germán said, leaning back so I could hear above the bus's roar and rattle. There was thick smoke in our wake and inside the bus was equally as thick with people, perspiring now from the heat of so many bodies pressed together. The children, with light in their eyes, were happy in the arms of their mothers. The old had dead looks, somber, like they had never seen Life or felt it. Or perhaps they had seen enough and were left without will. They had seen enough dust, delayed buses, hot sun and rain, and enough of the slow, monotonous pace, and were sick to death of the boredom.

In Villa Madero people shuffled to the front of the bus where they stepped off and others boarded. The pace was maddening. We started again and turned off the highway onto a tertiary road still some distance from La Purísima. I thought of Martín and realized he could easily hide or disappear in these small towns. Perhaps more easily here in the black mountains or in the remote villages, many of them nameless. I wondered how we would possibly find him. And if we did? Maybe I feared that more now

"It's the river," Germán said. "Up ahead is the

Carácuaro River. We follow it now to La Purísima." He revealed it to me like a tour guide.

Along the road, which was just packed earth now, were single homes or two or three clustered closely together. They were simple cement block structures with roofs of tarp or tin. Behind was the meandering river and long, green fields. A shade tree sprawled in front of each dwelling, only a few yards from the road. A eucalyptus tree or avocado, anything to get out of the midday heat. People stood along the roadside, old men and children waiting for something that never came.

Up ahead I noticed an enormous, deep pink bougainvillea stretching in front of a simple home. Green vines and beautiful flowers groped and twisted against concrete and tin.

"That's Jesús' home," Germán said.

What Jesús had told me was true. It was the largest and most beautiful bougainvillea I had ever seen. The most striking thing was the contrast, an elegant, colorful tree and the backdrop of colorless cement and tin—such beauty amidst poverty. The frail horse was tied to the tree out front, just as Jesús had described. The ribs were prominent; his coat was dull brown, without shine.

Germán held Hortencia very close to him now; the road was riddled with holes and the bus pitched and jerked. Her tender body was insulted each time we rolled through a hole or over a large rock in the roadway. For further protection, Hortencia's sister leaned ahead and gently placed her hands on Hortencia's shoulders. They treated her as if she were a fragile, newborn bird, each trying to beat out the other for the wrap or the helping hand.

"Too cold?" The wrap.

"Thirsty?" The water bottle.

"Too much sun?" The blanket.

"Too much air?" The window.

Soon the bus came to a sudden, lurching stop, stirring a swell of dust. When the dust cleared I could see we were near a plaza, where a cracked stone church stood, leaning slightly from age I assumed. It had a faded, blue tiled cupola and one cracked steeple. The plaza was nearly empty of people, just stone, scraggly trees, and sparse bushes. There were handfuls of townspeople lined up waiting to board the bus. They looked at me with suspicion in their eyes.

"We can walk to Hortencia's home," Germán said. "It's only a couple of blocks from here."

We walked slowly, nearly painfully so. Germán and the sister supported Hortencia on each side while I walked along deliberately behind them.

The town was cheerless and appeared uninhabited, though we saw a face or two in a doorway as we passed. In one were an old woman and a small child, the space behind them inky and bottomless.

"La Purísima," Germán said. "My home, *maestro*."

There were peeling political banners posted on street lamps and on the stone whitewashed walls lining the streets. The walls were painted with large bright campaign slogans. A presidential election was only weeks away and rival parties tried to outdo one another. We came to a door along the stone wall. There was a cement step and the pale burgundy door that met us was solid wood, with streaks, like deep gashes all the way down and tiny holes from termites dotted the wood. You would never guess that a home was behind that door.

The door opened and a girl, younger than both Hortencia and her sister, stood in the doorway. She appeared to be about twelve, though wore makeup, a navy blue dress with tiny yellow flowers on it and white sandals. She turned her head toward the vacant room behind her and announced Hortencia's arrival. We entered the room, which was narrow with a shiny tile floor. It was surprisingly cool inside and I was happy to be out of the sun. The house was spread out like a long rectangle; an oval dining table in the rear and a small garden was behind that.

"Hortencia!" a woman's voice called as she hurried down the stairs. "*Pobrecita*! My poor baby!" she hustled to embrace her.

"Careful, *mamá*," the sister cautioned her mother. "She is still very fragile." The two women swallowed Hortencia. Germán had no choice but to drift back from them. Immediately they began leading her to the stairs.

"Let's get you upstairs and into bed," her mother said. "My poor child. *Ay, mi reina*. What did that evil man do to my queen?" She then turned to Germán. "Thank you," she said sincerely, but as if there were more to say to him—not more gratitude, but something else. "I'm sorry to tell you that you may not see Hortencia again. Her father forbids it." There was an awkward silence.

"I'm sorry, Germán," she said, and the three sisters and their mother proceeded up the tiled stairway.

I expected Hortencia to protest her mother's words, but she was silent. Perhaps she was too tired from the trip home, but she didn't question her mother, who was perhaps only the messenger. Germán didn't question her either, out of respect, surprise, or simply awaiting his lover's protest that never came. The women disappeared up the stairs and we returned to the street.

"More reason now," Germán said. "More reason to avenge Hortencia and her family. It will be the only way her family will forgive me."

It was a two kilometer walk to Germán's home. Since we had arrived in La Purísima I had not seen a man over sixteen or under sixty. It was just as Jesús and Germán had told me; the entire town of working age men had gone north.

Along the way we stopped at Jesús' home. We found his sister and her husband, Magnolia and Salvador, tending to the small plot of land behind it. The bright bougainvillea lit up the front of the home, but the back was little more than mud and a small stone building. It was crumbling and looked like a mortar might have hit it.

"Dulce and the boys left a week ago," Magnolia told us. "First to Mexico City and from there I don't know. North is all I know." She pointed off in the direction the bus had taken them. "They will call into town when they arrive to Jesús."

From her words I could tell how little she knew of the world. She had probably never left La Purísima and had no idea about the North or anywhere else for that matter. The next town over was as big a mystery to her as Michigan. Salvador remained a distance behind her, like a second-class citizen.

When we left I asked Germán about Magnolia's husband. "Why is he still here? He looks young enough and healthy."

"Oh, Salvador is young and his body is healthy," Germán said. "But not his mind. There was an accident. He fell out of the back of a pickup truck a few years ago. He went headfirst. He's not much fit for work. He can tend to a small plot of land, but that is about it."

Germán led us back near the Carácuaro River.

"I played here when I was growing up. This river won't pose a threat like the one on the border. In the dry season it only trickles and is little more than an arroyo. It will lead us behind my home."

Up ahead two women squatted at the bank of the quiet river. Their skirts floated in the shallow waters while they washed clothes by hand with a rock and a large gold colored block of soap. The women scrubbed vigorously but didn't stir as we passed, tirelessly continuing the backbreaking work. We walked past them invisibly it seemed, without as much as a smile or turn of their heads. They silently urged Germán to leave.

"I know them," Germán said.

"But I know they saw you," I told him, unsure of the reason for the avoidance.

"I'm poison," he said. "You saw how Hortencia's family looked at me." I had and I noticed the way those women ignored him.

"They blame me for the attack on Hortencia," Germán said. "The attack is seen as a threat to the entire community. They don't want me here."

Germán was treated as a traitor, as a man who drew evil like a magnet, and attracted uncertainty to the community. Surely by now, the whole community had heard those words spoken by the stranger in the night, "this is for Germán." It seemed the town had become one, pulled together in passive solidarity in an effort to ostracize Germán. Perhaps to denounce him and label him the enemy, hoping to drive him away. But Germán's will was strong and he wouldn't allow it to happen. For one he wished to win Hortencia back, and too because he had nowhere else. La Purísima was all he knew. He had nowhere else to go. He knew La Purísima and its pace, its dusty streets, the meandering river, and the dull eyes reflecting the endless boredom and superstition.

We slept that night in the home of Germán's parents. The house, made of shoddy brick with a tin roof, was a distance from the main road. The river wasn't far behind it. Germán and I shared a room with two single beds. There was unreliable electricity in the home and despite the day's heat it was damp and cool inside. For warmth, I learned that the family would sit under the morning's warm rays, like reptiles. The home made you cold-blooded, so that nothing but the immediate air maintained your body's temperature. The night was cool and it rained. The clatter of raindrops on the tin roof was deafening and made it impossible to sleep until the early hours of the morning when the rain finally trickled away. Then we were left with a mighty chorus of insects and frogs.

Before we went to bed that night I found Germán removing a crucifix from above his bed. There were two rosaries draped over it. He carelessly shoved it under his bed.

"What are you doing?" I asked him, curiously.

"Keeping the evil spirits away. I don't want that God looking over me tonight. Your bed has one too. Do you want it down?"

"It's not important to me. Either way, I'll sleep the same," I assured him. "I'm not superstitious."

"Suit yourself, *maestro*," he said, before slipping under the covers.

IX

In the morning Germán's parents and his sister, Lilia, slithered out into the morning sun like cold-blooded things. Adjoining the back of the house was a stone patio where a mesh hammock hung and a circle of white plastic chairs were huddled. I walked out to the patio and then down to the riverbank. Tall grasses waved in the morning breeze and I could see the river had risen with the rain and flowed swiftly. Beyond the river was a grassy field glistening in the sun's rays, still damp from the wet night. The entire valley seemed to gradually come alive like it was being born, slowly warming, heating the land and its reptilian people. Germán joined me. I noticed a couple of areas in the nearby hills and mountains where smoke billowed.

"Why the smoke?" I asked.

"This region is ideal for marijuana growing. Those are the camps of the growers. Some could be from fugitives too," he speculated. "Men hiding from the law or just avoiding the world."

"Like Martín?" I asked.

"Maybe," he said as we both stared off into the black mountains. If a man wanted to hide here and never be found, he could do it.

A breakfast of tortillas, beans, and fruit awaited us at the house. We ate quickly and then started toward town. Germán insisted on walking on the main road, refusing to lurk in the shadows near the river. Despite the town's silent protest, he would walk in plain view, in the bright light of the day for anyone to see. We passed an elderly man on a burro, with a saddle of tightly bundled palm leaves. His face didn't change, as if he didn't see us. Germán seemed unfazed. His pride was strong.

We stopped at the town's single pharmacy. There was a phone inside and I went to call Jennifer. Germán hurried off to Hortencia's, hoping he could see her today. I got through to Jen's office, but she was in one of those all-important meetings of hers.

"Can she call you?" the rehearsed voice asked.

"No, I don't have access to a phone. Just tell her I called."

"Of course, sir." That was all.

There was a priest at the counter paying for stacks of paper and pens. He looked young, probably in his thirties, and very clean cut. He wore black pants and a black short sleeve shirt, with the white collar. His clothes were well pressed. He had wavy, dark brown hair. I walked outside and he followed.

"Good morning," he greeted me in English. He introduced himself as Father Gabriel.

"Paul Westin."

"Germán's friend?" he asked.

"How did you know?"

"This is a small town. Everyone is known here and people know things sometimes even before they happen." He laughed. "Where are you from?"

"Chicago."

"I spent two years there at a Xaverian seminary. I studied and worked in the community. What brings you here?"

I was surprised he didn't already know. "A visit."

"Looking for Martín?" I was quiet. I felt like the man was reading my mind or seeing through me.

"Not necessarily," I said. But he knew. I changed the course of discussion and asked where he had grown up.

"Here in Michoacán. In a town called Ciudad Hidalgo. I've been in La Purísima for two years now." I looked off toward the crumbling church.

"The parish needs some work," I said.

"It does, but we're a long way down on the state's project improvement list," he said dejectedly. "We don't have much political clout. But we make do."

"It's the same everywhere," I assured him.

We talked for a few minutes more and soon we noticed Germán making his way toward us.

"Well…" Father Gabriel started. "If you're looking for Martín, come see me. Come alone." He went off in the direction of the church. Germán reached me.

"Any luck?" I asked.

"None. They refuse to let me see her. Were you talking with Father Gabriel?"

"Small world. He lived in Chicago for a time."

"Don't trust him," Germán said. "You can't trust priests." I decided to keep Father Gabriel's words to myself.

We walked to the town square. It was well shaded by *tabachín* trees and scattered with hydrangea boasting enormous white and lavender flowers. We rested on an iron bench. The people shuffling past looked numb from tedium. What I felt most here was a timeless boredom, a boredom that had hung here forever like a disease that slowly eats away at will and energy. What remains is a careless town, motivated only to rise after the sun is sufficiently high, crawl to its warmth, reptilian like, and spend the day staring at the main road or plaza, waiting for something that will never come. Do they know it will never come? Unless they are waiting for Death with those stone eyes. No dreams, just the deliberate, lingering days, hot, then rainy, and the meandering Río Carácuaro breathing shallowly behind them. And the marijuana growers and fugitives in the surrounding mountains, all of it churning and turning like a timeless thing, uninterrupted or disturbed, perhaps until now.

The entire town was unsettled. The men had gone north and one of La Purísima's own had struck out at the community. They feared Martín, yet at the same time they felt pity for him. After all, he was their son. Strangely, they blamed Germán. Germán was the reason for Hortencia's attack and he was to blame. Martín was a son gone bad because of awful circumstances created by another of their own. But in the town's eyes, Germán was not deserving of the same pity.

On the surface Germán showed no sign of disturbance about the town's reaction. He had come all this way home before the end of the harvest just to tend to Hortencia. And his thanks were that he couldn't sit with her and help her mend. He could no longer see her. And the town, his own people, turned their backs on him. He didn't show or expose it, but in that inward place where all men keep things, there was growing distress.

Now anger burned away inside him. Perhaps in his eyes it was visible, a faint glimmer of the inferno that raged beneath his skin. A man treated with disdain his entire life simply for the dark color of his skin, his features, and the indigenous lineage that ran through his veins. The blood of the land, of his ancestors, the pumping of his heart and that timeless drum that beat inside him was louder now. His thoughts and all his rage focused on the missing man. Martín was the object of all Germán's anger and defiance, and I feared where that might lead. Germán, who had once been faithful, rejected God, and now his whole world rejected him.

Since there was no chance for Germán to see Hortencia and Martín was nowhere to be found in La Purísima, we left for Pátzcuaro. The town is famous during the days approaching the Day of the Dead celebration, but now it would be quiet and lazy. We boarded the bus in town on a day that was clear, nearly cloudless, spacious Michigan blue, only deeper. The seats around us were crowded and it was difficult to breathe in the fetid air. Children were alive while the adults slept with their eyes open, swallowed by their own pride, the same thing that made them stoic and ambivalent.

The countryside was dense and green; pine trees lined long stretches of highway while off in the distance were *nopales*, yucca, and eucalyptus trees. On the flat grounds near the highway were neatly trimmed fields where men and women hunched over, stiff and crooked, tending to the land the same way it had been done for centuries. A horse pulled a primitive plow with a man behind it guiding the laborious tilling.

We passed through several small towns, one no different from the other. All poor, accustomed to poverty and to a pace so deliberate and lazy. The road was winding with tight curves, then valleys, and then a climb. There were wooden, A-frame structures high in the hills, Bavarian-like, reminiscent of Hansel and Gretel, so unlike Mexico. Along the roadside was a wooden cross, draped with plastic flowers, and spoiled food at its foot. A loved one dead and buried –hit by a truck or lost control of a speeding car in a drunken frenzy. And as we neared Pátzcuaro, the sky changed. It began to rain.

In Pátzcuaro we were left near Plaza Vasco de Quiroga. It was large and handsome, framed by soft stone buildings with balconies draped with white and pale blue banners. A park with gardens was in the center of the square. A small marching band played at the opposite end of the plaza and a swarm of people followed.

"Corpus Christi," Germán said. "The procession is for the day of Corpus Christi." Soon it grew quiet as the band and people marched out of the square. We could hear the birds now, chirping in the trees in the center of the plaza. The music was faint in the narrow, broken streets across the way.

"I'll show you the house with eleven patios," Germán said. "It's a museum now."

We climbed a broken, cobblestone street; the walls painted white on top and burgundy on the bottom half. The streets were empty; shops were open and owners leaned in the doorways passing the day. A tourist rushed past, hurrying to the next shop. In a dark doorway, an ancient woman slept. I bought silver earrings for Jennifer. I was thinking of her now. It wasn't so much that I missed her, I just thought of her at work, at restaurants, and lying in the sun at the lakefront. Her taut skin more shiny now from the rays, more bronzed and beautiful. Her blue eyes transparent, yet never losing their intensity and their sense of expediency. I had been told my eyes were different. I understood. They were remote and empty sometimes as if they were missing something, wishing to see more I suppose. More Life or Love perhaps. Though eyes can lie can't they? Surely they can deceive and hide what is really in a man. They say that eyes don't lie. I don't believe it. Not that I believe in deceit; I don't. But I know it exists as readily as revenge. Eyes can be worn like a mask. The people of La Purísima had a look of insolence, and who knew what was behind that.

After the patios we went further up the steep, crumbling streets and approached a church.

"*La Virgen de la Salud*," Germán said.

"Of health?" He nodded, seeming to concentrate, as if thinking of Hortencia and of healing. Out front were merchants selling fruits and sweets. We walked between the rows; flies were thick through the place. A man sold pineapple slices speckled by black spots with transparent wings. The air was thick, almost impenetrable with the heavy scent of sweet fruits and candies. And the buzz of bees and wasps insulted our ears and flew around like fairies, assaulting the overripe fruits dripping with putrid juices. The air was sticky; the ground was sticky. I hurried along and at the corner we could see the lake in the distance. The sun peered through again, its rays like needles piercing the lake's surface. I pointed to it and Germán hurried up beside me.

"Let's go back to the plaza," he said. He was searching. We were both hungry and we began back down the three blocks, like stairs, toward the plaza. The vista overlooking the lake, with cobblestone streets and red clay roofs in the foreground, was charming. In the distance, the lake was gray and dormant and black mountains hugged it all around. Little white specks floated on the surface. We couldn't forget why we were here.

"I thought he might be here in Pátzcuaro," Germán said. He said it thoughtfully, looking off, elsewhere, his eyes moving rapidly as if he would see Martín's face in the pink stone or selling fruits or candy. "I talked to a woman in La Purísima who knew Martín. He used to talk of coming here to live and make his living fishing,"

"Has she seen him?" I asked.

"Not since he left for the North over a year ago. No one has seen him since." I didn't mention the priest. He had said to come alone and I wouldn't jeopardize his trust.

The plaza was nearly empty. We ate a lunch of chicken and cheese *quesadillas* and then returned to the square. We strolled along the cloisters where wooden tables and chairs were sold. They were painted in vibrant reds, purples and greens, with smiling faces of the sun and moon. And flowers made of corn stalks in colors I had never seen before, such Life, such bright color against the soft gray stone. Two young women passed us. Both were dark with full lips and their liquid eyes were big and sprouted long thick lashes.

"*Las morenas,*" Germán commented. "We call them that – dark and beautiful." We watched their hips sway until they disappeared at the corner of the square.

The faint call of the ragged band returned. Behind us, entering the plaza was the procession of Corpus Christi. A swarm of people and color led the march with the band in the rear. The band consisted of several players wearing aqua colored jackets and hats. They played brass instruments: tuba, trombone, trumpet, and a base drummer thumped along with two snare drummers on either side. Germán and I circled back out from under the cloister and into the open where we were afforded a clearer view of the passing procession. They were a disorganized bunch. No military drum corps in the world would accept any one of them.

Shortly before it reached us the procession halted and the marchers turned toward a balcony above. Three women leaned over to the crowd of about two hundred people. The band played and marched in place. The people shouted up to the women and waved their arms, smiling and calling.

"Here!" they called, desperate for the women's attention. A swirling heap of humanity and growing energy built before us. The women on the thin balcony above, dressed in clean white blouses and beautifully colored skirts and aprons, began to toss things out to the mass of gatherers below.

"*Aquí!* For me!" the crowd called. White

handkerchiefs, towels, and bags of grapes sailed over heads and outstretched arms. People leaped to secure an offering. I watched, the band played and the bass drum thumped, my heart beat faster and harder in my chest, the people grew unconscious.

What I noticed was that their eyes had changed. They were different now. They were no longer consumed with indifference. The eyes of the people were full of Life, Laughter, and Joy! Where was the insolence? The boredom? They had come alive and I too felt a vibration inside me—a calling or an awakening. Unthinking, I drifted into the mass of bodies. Intoxicated now, I stretched my arms and reached with all I had. I was in front now, just below the balcony. The full bosomed women, in those colorful aprons that hurt the eyes, continued to toss and smile and laugh. The crowd was frenzied, and I, the outsider, was among them. We were all alive, and perhaps only now were the masks dropped. The bodies around me were dark and sweaty, a stench rose up from all of us, toward the women, their faces painted like wooden dolls. Surrounding me were faces filled with the motion of Life, silver teeth, a disfigured face, and not a hint of stoicism. The masks had fallen! The drum beat on and vibrated my body and in my head a bell rang.

Then I caught the eye of one of the women from the balcony. I must have looked a fool there—light eyes and taller than the rest. A white handkerchief, like a white dove, like purity, fluttered from her dark hand. It caught a gust of fetid air and then sailed directly to my outstretched hand. I snatched the cloth like a trophy, like an emblem or certificate of Life. I felt triumph. On it was a delicately embroidered flowerpot with yellow and violet flowers. I glanced over and found Germán on the periphery of the crowd, searching the faces for Martín.

He was unaware of anything but the search. And then the balcony was empty.

The women were on the street again. The march resumed. I drifted back toward the center of the plaza, allowing the procession to pass. The three women from the balcony were in front leading the ragged congregation. They held up their long skirts and marched, then turned, circling like the march of time. Color and motion, stale air, and then a gust of sweet perfume went through. Turning, turning with full, raised skirts, like the passing of the seasons. One woman carried a basket of bread on her hip. A jester trotted up and feigned to steal it. All that remained was scattered papier-mâché and grapes smashed on the cobblestone. Germán and I stood together in the procession's hollow aftermath. He stared off blankly down the street.

"We'll never find him," he said dejectedly, like it was a fact, something he knew for certain. "I don't see how we can ever find him," he said again, his will waning. The procession had stolen it perhaps and drained him of his drive and volition. I had no way of knowing and had no answer, but anyway said that we would find him.

"We've just begun," I reminded him. "The lake," I remembered. "Maybe he fishes here," I said in an attempt to ignite hope. I felt alive now with a strange new lease on life. The bass drum still thumped inside me and in my head was a dizzying vibration. I stuffed the embroidered handkerchief in my pocket and we set off for the lake.

We arrived at a public area along the south end of the lake.

"Tourists don't come here," Germán said. "This is a place for the people. A populist area." I quickly understood.

There was a small boardwalk and down a steep, grassy embankment was Lake Pátzcuaro. In the distance we could see the island of Janitzio in the center of the lake, hazy, just a mound of black and a faint white statue of Morelos in the center. The mountains sloped down to the lakeshore. Below was a launch where several boats were docked. They were wooden vessels, draped with saggy cloth tops for protection from the glaring sun. The men waited with their boats for hire—no takers. Germán scampered down to talk to them and inquire about Martín. I walked along the boardwalk shooing flies. In the lake's center, barely visible in the shimmer, were fishermen casting wide butterfly nets. Along the edges of the lake, tall grasses waved in the warm breeze. In their gold bunches they looked like hairs of corn, like silk thrashing in the afternoon sun.

Near me, a woman sat beside an overflowing basket of drying *charales*, a small fish taken from the lake. They looked like slender, transparent shards of glass, smothered with the persistent black flies. Germán came up the embankment, looking dejected.

"Nothing," he said. "None of them has seen anyone resembling Martín. Let's get out of here," he said and began to walk away from the lake. I followed and we passed through a narrow path lined on each side with long wooden benches. Women sat tightly together along them, still, and asleep with their eyes open. Small children scurried around the concrete, crawling on hands and knees in the filth. Several stray dogs trotted about. They looked like they had the mange. No one cared, even a little. The women had a look that said time meant nothing. In their eyes was indifference and an absent look, not boredom, but something else. I thought of Jennifer. She could not be here. She wouldn't tolerate this place: the offensive odors, the flies, and the heavy air, stale and murky. She would never survive here. Never.

I asked Germán if he had been here with Hortencia.

"Once I was. We sat there," he said, pointing to a nearby bench. "We took a boat to the island. The water was rough that day and Hortencia got sick to her stomach." He grinned, his face lighting up again from the memories. "It must have been from all the *charales* she ate. She loved them with drops of *chile*. They are fresh here by the lake, just caught and dried in the sun. Crisp, you know, *maestro*?"

"I've seen them."

We left Pátzcuaro and returned to La Purísima. When we arrived we went directly to Jesús' home. We hoped to hear the news that the family had arrived safely in Michigan. They had. Magnolia had received the news yesterday.

"There is something else," she told us.

"What is it?" Germán asked nervously.

"Follow me." Her husband Salvador stood behind her in the dim room. The couple led us out back of the house and along the edge of the cornfield. The morning was warming, but the grass was still damp. The air was consumed with a constant and heavy buzz. Salvador slowed and then circled around a clump in the grass. I could see the swarm of flies now, buzzing and circling the mound in the tall, wet grass. What we found was a mess of fur and flesh, limp and lifeless. Insects attacked the carcass unmercifully. It was one of Jesús' dogs. The other dog had followed us out and he stood still, tilting his head and staring at what was left of his comrade.

"It happened two nights ago," Magnolia explained. "We never heard a thing. We found that ground hoe there lying next to the dog, all full of blood and fur." The ground hoe was leaned against a nearby tree.

"I think it's Martín," Salvador said.

"Why didn't you bury the dog?" Germán asked without hesitation.

"We wanted you to see it," Magnolia answered. "To make sure it was Martín."

"Bury it," Germán instructed. "It's a hazard."

"Where?" Salvador asked. He was accustomed to direction, given instruction from his wife or from others, whoever was around to do it.

"Over there, along the tree line," Germán told him. "Not too close to a tree trunk, you'll hit root." Salvador went around front to grab a shovel.

"Did you tell Jesús about the dog?" Germán asked Magnolia.

"No, I didn't talk to him. We were given the message at the pharmacy."

"I'll talk to him. I'll call the orchard. He should be there for a few more days, but the harvest will be over soon." Germán and I turned back toward the house. Salvador passed us clutching a shovel, his head down, determined to do his job.

"A meter deep," Germán said. "No more, no less."

Out front of the house, near the main road, an occasional car passed.

"I need to leave for a couple of days," Germán told me. "There is another lake up north near Guanajuato and I want to check there. Can you stay at my parent's home?"

"Shouldn't I go with you?"

"No, it's best if you stay. Keep an eye on the place." I didn't persist and here was my chance to speak with Father Gabriel alone. I told Germán that I understood.

We walked toward town. When we reached the pharmacy Germán asked to use the phone. He dialed the orchard in Michigan. Jesús was nearby and came to the phone.

"Yes, it's Germán." He spoke loudly into the receiver like the connection was bad. "And Dulce and the boys? Yes, I heard they arrived." Germán told him about the dog.

"No, it's not evil. It's Martín. I'm sure of it. Hortencia and the dog—he's striking out at both of us. No, I wouldn't tell the *machitos* about the dog. No reason." Germán finished and then was silent for a few moments.

"No, it isn't a ghost, Jesús. It's the man in the flesh. Pray all you want, but I don't see what good it will do. I'm leaving tomorrow for a few days, maybe to the sierra. He must be there somewhere and I'll find him." Germán hung up the phone.

X

In the morning Germán was gone. The sun's rays were streaming in the bedroom's small window, spraying brightly on the wall above his bed, highlighting the hole where the crucifix had been. The room was bare. It had a rough concrete floor and several rugs were thrown. It was possible to walk from the bed to the kitchen without touching the clammy concrete with bare feet and that alone was a luxury.

Before going to the kitchen I lay still in bed, staring across the gray room and listening to birds' long shrieks and chatter outside the window. Each morning, regardless of whether it had rained during the night, the room felt damp. It was like a thirsty sponge sucking up every drop of moisture. In the corners of the room the cement had given way to moist, packed dirt. From the bed, the dank corners seemed far away and all around the stone walls wept gently. My only thought was to escape to the dry heat of the patio. The rest of the family was asleep.

Through the kitchen was a small patio where simple clay flowerpots were set and two clotheslines were strung across, full of drying clothes washed earlier at the river. I recognized some of my clothes. Someone had washed them. I brushed back a muslin shirt and walked toward the rear of the patio. Out back were the lush and the green. Brown, spiny lizards stuck to stone walls in places, warming, and when I drew too close they would scamper off into dark cracks and crevices. In the rear the land bent and then dropped off like a table the way an ocean floor does when the water becomes instantly deep. The constant here was the mountains in the distance, forever looming over this poor valley like a curse. A hummingbird zoomed around a nearby bush, then hovered just above its leaves for a few moments. Then there was a thud and the startled hummingbird zipped away like an insect. An avocado had fallen from a tree. I picked it up and set it on the edge of the patio. It was soft and spongy. For a moment, I admired the silence and simplicity. I hadn't breathed in this much clean, quiet air in a long time. I sat in the sun and felt the dry, prickly heat seep under my skin.

The shower was out on the patio and I decided to clean up before the others were out of bed. The shower was inconspicuously tucked away in a corner of the patio. The shower floor was dirt, so a wooden palette had been put in place to stand on. I still wasn't used to a cold shower, but Germán's mother assured me it was much healthier than a warm one. "Good for the circulation," she had told me. "Wakes the heart up in the morning too." The truth was she had known nothing else. I hoped my heart didn't require waking.

I stepped cautiously onto the wooden palette and closed the opaque plastic sheet behind me. I held my breath and pulled at the lever and a gush of ice cold water fell over me. I released it. Every pore on my body closed angrily and my extremities retracted against my stiff body. The soap didn't lather much, though I was thankful, because it would take less water to rinse. After soaping I reached again for the lever, counted to three and held my breath and released the stream. I let out a muffled scream while working the thin film of soap off my body. Afterward, I was back out on the patio clean and refreshed. My heart seemed to beat quicker, like it was more youthful now.

In the kitchen Germán's parents were at the table and his sister Lilia was preparing breakfast. She had a bowl of fresh eggs on the counter and turned to me when I came in the room.

"Coffee?" she asked.

"Please."

"Do you like eggs?"

"Of course. Thank you."

Germán's father pulled a chair out from under the small table. He had the same bushy eyebrows as his son, though grayed. Awkwardly, I sat down. Lilia's parents were older. She either had older siblings or the couple had had Germán and Lilia later in life. I remembered my clothes on the line out back and I looked to Germán's mother.

"Thank you for washing my clothes. You really didn't..."

She cut in, "it was Lilia."

"Oh, Lilia, then thank you," I said rather clumsily.

Lilia was at the stove scrambling the eggs with one hand resting on her hip and the other clutching a spatula.

She didn't turn around, allowing my eyes to sweep her body momentarily. The morning light washed over her and I could now see her figure and the way her long black hair fell over her brown shoulders. She wore a simple, cotton dress that hung loosely, except for hugging her full hips. I must have stared at her for a few moments, for I seemed to lose my senses.

"Do you want *chile*?" her mother asked me. I must have looked empty because she clarified.

"For your eggs?"

"Not necessary," I replied dumbly.

We ate and afterward Germán's parents and Lilia slithered out to the front of the house in search of the morning sun. Like lizards they found it and bathed in its warmth. Out the front window of the house I gazed at Lilia. She was sitting on a blanket spread in the grass. She leaned to one side and gently ran her hand along the length of her shining calf. Her skin looked smooth and soft, and despite the modest surroundings I could tell she took special care of herself. Her face was thin, not dull, but lustrous and her eyes were almond shaped like the Mayans, and above them grew fine eyebrows. I recalled what Germán had said; Poverty is not a crime. I left out the back patio and strolled down to the river. I would follow it into La Purísima for a visit with Father Gabriel.

The river ran slow that morning and washed over rocks and smoothed its silken banks. Polished rocks peered up like glistening globes, each a universe. I wondered how the men of La Purísima react when they first lay eyes on the Río Grande if all they have ever seen is the meager Río Carácuaro. This river was just a playground for children. Up ahead two of them were playing, dressed only in underwear. When they saw me they stopped and stared blankly, in surprise or amazement. My light eyes seemed to unsettle people. Along the bank there were footprints in the mud where women had washed clothes or bathed. The river stretched along the edge of La Purísima and followed it upstream to the northeast corner of the town where the church was. The church sat on the north end of the plaza and looked down to the river. It was a simple stone structure and at least on the outside was not garnished like other churches I had seen in Mexico. The narrow river was all that separated the church from the base of the mountains.

Inside, the church was simple smooth stone, open and airy. The altar was ornate; there was a large crucifix on the wall behind it and Christ's body was smeared with gore. Boxes with glass fronts were mounted on the sides protecting statues of saints that looked like children in velvety gowns. Gold leaf accented each piece of furniture and against the simple structure the altar looked obscene, almost vulgar. Candles were lighted on the communion table and the room smelled of incense and felt damp from the cement floor. From the end of the nave, I studied the authentic appearance of the crucifix: the blood the color of blood and flesh the color of my own. I reminded myself that the ornamentation was not for my eyes, but for the eyes of the faithful.

"Don't you see the love in those eyes?" Father Gabriel asked from the doorway.

"I only see pain, Father," I said.

"Well, you've come," he said. "I was beginning to wonder."

"We'd gone to Pátzcuaro to search for Martín."

"You won't find him there," the priest said. I walked slowly toward him.

"Where will we find him?" I asked. Father Gabriel skirted the question and asked about Germán.

"He's not here. He's gone to search for Martín further north or in the sierra," I told him.

The priest led me to an adjoining room where it appeared he lived. He ran his fingers through his thick, wavy hair. In one corner were a bed and an armoire, and a simple table rested next to the bed. Tall piles of paper were stacked neatly around the nightstand. In the center of the room was a rectangular table, painted antique blue, with six chairs around it. It was cluttered with papers.

"Do you live here?" I asked him.

"Yes."

"And how did you end up in La Purísima?"

"Just luck," he joked, affording me his humanity. "I was born in Ciudad Hidalgo here in Michoacán, the youngest of five sons. My father was a barber. My mother had promised she would give one of her sons to God. When I turned eighteen we all looked at each other. Well, I was the only one left. Of course it was my choice," he assured me. "I wouldn't have it any other way."

"I read a novel like that once," I said. "But the protagonist left the seminary after falling in love. Machado de Assis, I believe."

"I never fell in love," the priest said, before walking to a window and peering into the morning. "At eighteen I was sent to a Xaverian seminary in Mexico City. I spent five years there. After Mexico I spent three years in Guadalajara with a group of Italian priests and then two years in Chicago. After that directly to La Purísima to become the head priest. Actually, the only priest," he said with a gentle smile.

"Who did she make the promise to?" I asked curiously. He turned to me with a puzzled look. "Your mother – who did she make the promise to about you becoming a priest?"

"To God," he answered. "She promised God."

We sat down at the table and Father Gabriel brought coffee. I commented on the presidential election coming in a week and asked for his opinion.

"Michoacán will be the only state that votes PRD. But the vote is for the father, not the son," he said.

"And change this time?"

"Perhaps," he began. "It's time after seventy-one years. The PAN is gaining support, but I suspect there will be no difference. Where did you meet Germán?" he asked.

"At an orchard while doing research for my doctorate."

"What school?" the priest asked.

"University of Chicago."

"The mission in Chicago was very near to the university," he said. "Hyde Park."

"That's my neighborhood," I said.

"What other men do you know?"

"Many from La Purísima, but I know Germán and

Jesús the best," I told him.

"We had a Mass for Jesús' family two Sundays ago. We prayed for a safe journey to Michigan."

"It must have worked," I said. "They arrived safely." I told the priest about the dog that had been killed. He had already heard.

"I told you," he said. "Some things are known even before they happen."

I was eager to get to the point of my visit. "What do you know of Martín?" I asked. "And why did you ask me to come alone?" He didn't speak right away.

"I'm afraid," he answered. "Afraid for both Martín and Germán. And for La Purísima too, I suppose. The town needs to heal. We have a marker out back for Benito. His body was never found. Many blame Germán for his death. Martín blames him, but he also blames himself. He is ashamed to ever show his face here."

"Have you seen him?" I asked.

"I have. I saw him about three months ago for the first time since he left for the North. Since then he has come a couple of times. The last time was two weeks ago." The priest drank from his coffee. His hands were smooth and clean.

"Where have you seen him?" I asked.

"Here at the church. He comes late at night when the town is asleep. He comes from the mountains."

"He lives in the mountains?"

"Yes, he spent time with some growers up there, but has his own camp now."

"Growers?"

"Marijuana," he said. "The mountains here are ideal for its growth." The priest asked me what I wanted with Martín.

"Nothing. I came at Germán's request," I said. "He was numb after hearing about what had happened to Hortencia. Germán didn't say it right away, but I think he knew it was Martín."

Next Father Gabriel asked me what I thought Germán wanted with Martín.

"Simply to stop him, I think. He came here for Hortencia, to see her well again. But now her parents refuse to let Germán see her." There was a pause.

"But isn't it really revenge that Germán wants?" Father Gabriel asked me, leading me with the question. "Isn't it as basic and awful as that?" I didn't answer.

"Shouldn't the law be involved?" I finally asked. "Isn't this a matter for the police or a court of law?"

"There is no rule of law in La Purísima. We have never had a need."

"Maybe now there is a need," I said.

"And you? Are you sure you're not here for another reason? Hiding or running from the law or someone?" he asked.

"No, it's part of my doctoral dissertation," I told him.

That was it, I thought. Professor Lassene had encouraged it perhaps only for vicarious reasons. And Jennifer – I had no reason to run from her, from our love and upcoming marriage. I had come for a friend and for my profession. That was all.

"All I want is peace and reconciliation. I want to bring

Martín and Germán together. It's the only way. The only way to mend La Purísima," Father Gabriel said.

I stared into my coffee cup during an uncomfortable silence. I'm not sure why I said it, maybe to fill the awkward void, but the words just fell from my lips. I don't even recall thinking them.

"I think I can help, Father," I said. "Let me talk to Martín first, before Germán does. Perhaps I can help bridge the two. I know Germán and I know the story of the drowning at the river."

"You know *Germán's* story," Father Gabriel reminded me.

"Yes, but I may be of some help," I said, persistent in something I hadn't given much conscious thought to. "Let me talk to Martín," I pleaded.

I suppose it was because I had carried Martín with me somehow, ever since I had heard the recounting of the river crossing. I had never seen Martín, but I pictured the man, on the run, unable to return home, living in the shadows, lurking, never knowing how to right things. Never quite knowing how to even the score or to avenge his brother's senseless death, yet feeling compelled to. It had taken him over a year to devise a plan to strike at the pure—La Purísima. In his mind, surely the whole town was at fault. The entire miserable rite of passage. Father Gabriel explained to me that Martín had never wanted to go. He never wanted to leave La Purísima. But it was the way now for young men. The burden was thrust upon him; he'd never asked for it.

Father Gabriel was quiet. He looked at me seriously, then rubbed his hands vigorously together, as if he were trying to spark a fire. I could see he was contemplating. Finally he agreed to a meeting.

"But it must be the three of us: you, Martín and me. Of course Martín will have to agree to the meeting," he said. I understood.

"We will need to meet soon," I told him. "Germán will be back in a day or so."

"My altar boy knows where Martín's camp is. Come by tomorrow afternoon," Father Gabriel told me.

It was hot and dry now as I walked through the streets of La Purísima. We had not seen rain in a couple of days. As always, the town seemed deserted, or nearly so. A head would peer from a doorway then instantly dart back when I glanced in its direction. La Purísima had only a few streets, stone, broken paths where few people walked. Rather they would scurry from place to place, hiding and lurking on the margins as if light would harm them. I wondered if this is how the town had always been, joyless and ghostly. It was as if some imminent darkness loomed, like a bad omen, invisible, but the entire town felt it hanging over them, sucking them of even a sliver of energy. It seemed all but the children were consumed by it. Had it always existed here or was it Benito's drowning? Had the haunting fear of one of their own created this lethargy, this shifty eyed hiding, and deceptive calm? The stagnation and silence was excruciating. I hated the stillness! Man is not meant to live this way.

The fear that gripped this place made me uneasy. The few eyes that I had seen were frozen, black superstitious marbles, void of Life. In all of them was simply the long wait for Death. I thought of Pátzcuaro and the lively procession. Perhaps that is the only time when a town and its people come alive. A time when the reptiles crawl from their cool, dank caverns and slither to the streets and march, turn and stretch. It is the only time when Life is permitted and that looming gray, that constant call of Death recedes and joy takes hold. Masks fall and people drift together as one hopeful mass of dizzying humanity. People laugh and dance, and the town's soul is cleansed, released from hibernation, and returned to its original chaste self. All is permitted in the frenzy of the procession and of the fiesta. Release! A communal letting go ensues and people feel again and float in the air's weightlessness. Even the air thins and the thick scents and dense, heavy blanket of living Death dissipates and allows for a respite, for Life to grasp hold again, wrestled from Death's sinewy arms.

There were few businesses in La Purísima. Other than a dentist and a barber, there was the pharmacy, a *panadería*, a *tortillería*, a hardware store, and little else. I had nearly passed an open doorway when I noticed the painted words on the whitewashed stone wall beside it: Cyber-café. Inside I found a young man, probably in his early teens, behind a counter thumbing through a magazine. He was slender with deep-set eyes.

"Good afternoon," I said. He said the same and then informed me with some excitement, "the server is up." I asked him if that was unusual.

"It depends," he said. "It's sporadic and if we have problems it can take days to fix. The technician comes from Villa Madero."

"I'll consider this my lucky day then." The café offered coffee, so I ordered a cup and sat at one of the two computers. Since I hadn't spoken to Jennifer this was the next best thing. I hurriedly wrote her a note. It was cryptic and hasty, but I feared the server would crash.

Will be longer than expected. All is fine. Sorry I

missed the fittings. Miss you.

That was all. How impersonal, I thought, but all I had at the moment. The boy brought the coffee. It was lukewarm; I drank it anyway. I hid out there in the cool shade, loitering, hesitant to return to the fiery stone and sun outside.

The sun was high now and finally I set out for the house by way of the river. I felt a strange lethargy and I strolled thoughtlessly, almost in a sleepy playfulness. Perhaps it was the heat. The path was familiar now and I anticipated the meager bridge made of wood and rope that crossed the water and just beyond it the sharp bend in the river. I felt I knew it now. The sound of tracing water, a soothing lullaby, and I peered up through the leafy trees, almost mocking the sun for it couldn't reach me under the rich canopy of foliage. In places, the canopy disappeared and a dry grassy field spanned before me. I drew a deep breath before submerging again into the dampness of the heavily tree-lined lengths of the river.

Sometimes there were fences in the open fields. The style I found most often and admired were the low, stone fences built of individual rocks laid by hand. The rock was soft, brown or black stone piled up two feet high or so. The piled rocks formed a winding perimeter designed to prevent small herds of cattle from wandering beyond their boundaries. The fences had been erected with noticeable care and patience. They were so unlike anything else here that was done with such carelessness and not an ounce of precision.

XI

Before long I was back at the house. I was tired and sat in a plastic chair on the patio. I read for a while, looking up often to gaze at the open behind me and inhale the fertile ground of Mexico. I thought of the gods that once reigned in Mexico and imagined in some remote, isolated places, they still did. The sky swept quickly overhead. The clouds' shadows washing over the mountains. At times it looked like the mountains were moving, shifting, or floating along the horizon. And then a light, a flicker or reflection in the far off hills. Martín? I wondered. Or Germán climbing, scouring the mountain paths for his revenge? And if he found Martín? I could only shudder. Yet it was unlikely since the sierra was vast, endless it seemed, and rugged. But if he did? There would be a fight and perhaps a death, another senseless death for La Purísima to swallow. I doubted that the town would survive another.

Lilia walked out on the patio. She wore a bright yellow smock and her hair was pulled up. Her skin glistened in the sharp rays. I was sitting where she wouldn't notice me, concealed by drying clothes on the line. She went to the shower; her feet found the wooden palette and she closed the plastic curtain. Next the yellow smock sailed over the curtain and was caught by a wooden hook. The sound of running water came trickling and crackling. I could see her ankles and copper colored feet beneath the curtain and I watched them become soaked, glistening in the water's gentle rush. Her body's silhouette wasn't visible through the curtain's opacity, but I imagined it. Her copper glazed body dense with the scent of earth. I imagined these things... the curved lines beneath her breasts, her neck arched, straight and majestic, her modesty, gazing up at the clear liquid chasing between her breasts and then down her burning thighs. Lilia's eyes now closed, her thick lashes damp, cradling a droplet of water like a pearl, her back arched now, sure to receive every sprinkle. What a crime to waste a drop.

As I watched and imagined her, I thought of every woman I had ever loved. I conjured up what sediment remained from their memory, some faint and others not at all. For some, it was just a face, or the way she looked at me, her eyes, or her authentic laugh, or her voice. And one, it was just a slender, olive colored hand on top of mine. How strange memory is. When you hunger for it, desperately reaching, it isn't there. When required most it hides in exile. But at moments like this when it isn't needed or even sought, here it comes for all it's worth like a tidal wave. The flash of an eye, a once gentle touch, a phrase, or a long ago whisper, and the smiles and all the wistful adolescent sensations that man experiences in new love have come again. All at once they wash over us, and we brace ourselves from their maddening rush wherever we might be. Is it in a subway, at a café, in Mexico, on a burning patio in the shadows of the song of trickling water? I told myself to listen – to the whisper of the river, to the earth, the shower's crackle, the night's rain, and to my own throbbing heart.

Lilia emerged from the shower on tiptoes. Once again her body draped in the loose yellow smock, her hair damp and straight. She sat in a plastic chair like my own and snatched a porous rock she had placed there earlier. With the pumice stone she began rubbing gently over the bottoms of her feet, smoothing over the soles and heels to erase the thickening and the hardening required for the feet to survive. Perhaps there is such a stone for the heart or for the soul. A stone that would peel away the thick, hard layer of Life and superstition that surrounds the heart like a cocoon's protective shell. Perhaps the soul's porous stone is memory. In moments of solitude, memories waft in, unsolicited and bathe man's soul, cleansing it of impurities. The heart feels again and recalls all those tender moments, the very memories that a protective shell has shut out and holds far away. Brace yourself! They've washed up on shore— old loves, old lovers, flashes of each, like a runaway thing...

Lilia finished and returned to the house. For now I had finished reading and dreaming. I grew tired and drowsy. The heat, the walk to town, and the boredom now rocked me, gently rocking, my head bobbing and nodding. I fell asleep.

* * *

The next afternoon I arrived at the church. Father Gabriel was waiting for me and hurried us into his quarters and shut the door behind.

"The boy reached Martín," he told me, almost in a whisper. "Martín came here last night and he's agreed to meet you. Though, on the condition that I'm present and we meet here at the church." I quickly agreed to the simple conditions.

"I think Martín is tired now," Father Gabriel said. "He's wearing down and I believe he wants peace. I told him the survival of La Purísima depends on it."

"If he's weary then why the attack on Hortencia? Only two weeks ago, Father?"

"Martín asked for Hortencia last night. He asked about her condition and he wept in my arms. I told him God would forgive him. He *will* be forgiven." Father Gabriel held out open hands before him, as if he was cradling an infant. "We need peace now," he said with urgency in his voice. His jaw tightened as he spoke.

I noticed a man's portrait on the wall. He appeared to be another priest but with uncharacteristic ferocity in his eyes. He looked more revolutionary than ecclesiastical, yet he wore the unmistakable collar. Father Gabriel noticed me eyeing the portrait.

"Do you know that man?" he asked.

"I don't."

"That's Father José María Morelos," he said proudly. "He was one of the leaders of Mexican Independence. You must have seen his statue on the island of Janitzio when you went to the lake. Morelos was born here in Michoacán and was a priest at a parish in Carácuaro, along the river. He's a hero in our nation's history, especially here in Michoacán. He and Don Vasco de Quiroga are two of the most prominent men from our state."

I had heard of Morelos and remembered the significant role priests played in the history of Mexico, especially in the independence movement. It was logical then that the only contact Martín had made with La Purísima was through the town parish. Father Gabriel, he knew, would not betray him.

"I don't condone what Martín did," the priest said. "On the contrary, he will face God's judgment. But he is a merciful God and has already forgiven Martín. We need to do the same."

"Martín will also need to forgive," I said. "He'll need to let go of the hate and blame he holds for Germán."

"Hate is ugly," the priest said, his eyes searching the wall and looking at the face of Morelos, determined now. "It can only destroy," he said soberly. "We need peace and forgiveness. Pray for it," he said as he turned to me.

"Forgiveness is difficult. We're only human," I reminded him.

"Then pray," he said.

I didn't respond. "When will we speak to Martín?"

"Tonight. Come back tonight after dark."

I walked back toward the house, along the river again, hidden as much as possible. I stopped at Jesús' home on the way. Magnolia and Salvador were there.

"We buried the dog," she told me.

"Good," I replied, filling in the words reserved for Germán. I felt I was taking his place, acting as he would, strong and direct. The couple asked for him. "He's gone searching for Martín. Up near Lake Cuitzeo or in the sierra."

"Hope he finds him," Salvador said. His hands balled into mighty fists and at his temples, transparent flesh pulsated, like his heart skipped wildly at the thought of finding Martín. Like a boxer, his broad, thick shoulders circled the air. "If I found him," he began again with bulging eyes fixed on the ground. He hadn't finished when Magnolia burst in.

"Hush!" She scolded him like a child. "You have no part in this!" He quieted.

I felt for the man. He was a man physically. He was strong and worked hard I could see. But that day he was injured his mind had been arrested and then cruelly deported to childhood. He was just an impulsive boy and perhaps angry at times, while desperately searching for approval. Sadly it was an approval that never came. His wife was clever and she liked it that way. She enjoyed the fact that Salvador forever tried to please her, but never allowed him to succeed. I asked about Jesús. Magnolia had spoken with him.

"The harvest is over," she said. "He's started a factory job now and they've moved to an apartment."

"Good," I said. Jesús' dream was beginning. He must be happy, I thought. "And the boys?" I asked. The boys who I had never met or seen, but who I felt I knew. I had heard so much about them and when I did I felt something like an uncle's pride.

"Samuel is in school now," she said.

"In the summer?" I asked.

"Oh, he has to learn English. And Pepito, he only cries they say. He cries when Samuel goes off to school."

"He must want to go too," I said.

"He'll get his chance, but he's little now. We all get our chance sooner or later," she said, as if referring to something else. Salvador, who had been listening intently, spoke up.

"When will Germán return?" he asked in his monotonous tone, never inflection or mood.

"Soon I would guess. Maybe in a day or two." He filed the information away.

It was late afternoon. The sun rested on one of the thousand mountain peaks. The day was drowsy and still. The air listless, not a leaf or branch stirred as I walked back to the house. When I arrived Lilia was there and she asked me if I had eaten. I hadn't. She fixed me something.

"I heard Hortencia's father forbids Germán to see her," she said. "Is it true?"

"I'm afraid it is."

"I don't understand." She looked confused. "He left his work because of her. It isn't fair."

"Not everything is fair," I said. She knew that as well as anyone. "When you expect justice and don't get it, that's when it is the most difficult," I said. Lilia agreed. "If you expect something and it never comes, that's when you feel injustice the most."

"I suppose it's like anything else," she began. "If it comes and goes away, maybe you feel it more. I expected something at one time."

"What was it?"

"I expected to get out of here," she said coldly.

"Out of this house? Out of this town?" I asked.

"Both. Out of this house and out of La Purísima," she said, as if I understood, or should have.

"Where did you want to go?"

"To Morelia. I wanted to become a nurse."

"It's not too late," I said stupidly.

Lilia laughed at me. "What do you know?" she said. "It's too late now, maybe it was always too late." She was right. I knew nothing of her life.

"No, I must stay here now. My brothers are gone and my parents are getting older. Germán is only here half the year, and well..." She stopped. I nodded my head as if I understood now.

Lilia brought me a plate with a thin slice of beef and a spoonful of rice.

"I'll warm the tortillas," she said.

"Thank you for having me in your home."

"You're Germán's friend, aren't you?"

"I am."

"Well," she said.

"Did you want to become a nurse so you could help people?" I asked.

"Not so much that," she admitted. "More or less it's practical. And good work for a woman."

"You're a pragmatist then," I commented jokingly.

"If you say so," she said.

"Don't be offended. They make the world go round."

I wanted to ask her about a boyfriend or lover, but didn't. I thought it shallow and besides she was my friend's sister. And if I hadn't forgotten, I was engaged to marry. Lilia brought steaming tortillas, wrapped neatly in a colorful towel. She sat with me while I ate. It was customary, but awkward.

XII

That evening, after it had grown dark, I slipped out onto the back patio and groped for the river. The night was black and still, as if in restrained anticipation. I couldn't see the river, but heard it as I approached. My stomach felt raw and tight as I began to navigate along the river's bank. The insects' call, shrill and native, rang in my head. I breathed heavily in my own private fear of meeting the fourth man. As I walked, I thought of the man who had grown almost mythical to me. Yet I would see him in the flesh and sit across the table. What would I say? I only wanted to hear his story.

None of this was of any value to my dissertation. None of this mattered really. It was too personal for that, simply the insignificant trials of so few men. Wasn't this the truth of it? The angry, miserable truth of what economic disparity will bring? The truth boiled up now between statistics and words, without pathos, without an ounce of feeling. Who cared after all? Professor Lassene knew. This is what he wanted for me and why he wanted me to come to Mexico. To see and experience first hand, to inhale Life and embrace it. I loved him now and I felt him with me on the path of the Río Carácuaro. It wasn't vicariousness as I had expected. I seemed to understand now his gentle urge for me to come to La Purísima. Perhaps the truth of it all was here and I would hear it tonight with my own ears, just as he surely had, under different circumstances, years ago in Africa.

I thought that this is the unfortunate reality of economic disparity. When a poor country sleeps next to a rich country and the poor roll over to the other side, but all the while they can't wait to return. This is what happens when the poor cross over and work for the rich, sleep in their beds and eat their food. When a town sacrifices all of its young men and a town becomes consumed by its own poverty, a victim of itself, a wound inflicted by its own desperate hand. And now, two men wanting to destroy it, to stamp it out and negate it like it never existed. To kill each other's souls, to kill La Purísima, the pure, implode it into dust and return it to what it was in pre-Hispania—an innocent plain of greenery and dust, mud, and waving grasses.

Eventually I reached the church. The sky was black, without stars or moon, just a low, velvet blanket of night sky. The air began to stir. A storm brewed just beyond the mountains. I went around to the back of the church and noticed a glowing white hue from one window. It was the room where Father Gabriel slept. Inside the church the door to his room was slightly ajar and I eased up and peered in. Father Gabriel was alone, sitting at the table in the center of the room, writing. On the table, a lamp was lit, illuminating the room's center. The periphery remained in shadow. When I knocked on the door he quickly turned and rose from the table to greet me. I thought I saw disappointment in his eyes when he realized it wasn't Martín.

"Has Martín arrived?" I asked him.

"Not yet," he answered, turning back toward the table. We sat across from one another. The lamp's reflection burned in his eyes. He wasn't wearing the collar. Instead he wore a snug fitting white T-shirt. There were papers on the table and he began to straighten them.

"Were you writing?" I asked.

"Yes, letters. I'm behind on my letter writing. Late at night is when I write them while the town sleeps. The only interruption is a storm, or Martín, or a late night clandestine confession, as if God can't see at night." It began to thunder and weak lightning flashed inside the room.

"Is he coming?" I asked, finding worry in the priest's face.

"He'll be here," he said confidently.

It was raining now. At first it was steady, but quickly it turned into a driving rain. I thought of the river and how it would grow in depth and width, eager to fill out its rightful property. And then, without introduction or warning, Martín stood inside the room. His face was hidden in the darkness, until a flash of lightning came, and for a second he was lit up like an actor on a stage. Martín walked slowly toward the table and as he drew closer we could see he was drenched. His hair was soaked and matted to his head and he wore a beard dripping water from its fringes.

"Let me get you a towel," Father Gabriel said, hurrying off to fetch one.

We stared at one another for a few moments. Martín was a wiry man. He wore dark colored jeans and a long sleeved light denim shirt that was soaked through. There was stiffness about him. A belt was wrapped around his waist that looked like it could have made it around him another time.

"Come sit down," I finally said, and he sank into the chair across from me.

"You are Germán's friend?" he asked, suspicious like, but without threat. I told him I was.

"We met in Michigan."

"Whcrc is he now?" he asked.

"Looking for you." It seemed like a long time, but Father Gabriel finally returned with a towel. Martín dried his head and face and then draped the towel around his neck. Below his Adam's apple was a hollowed depression, everyone had one, but his was especially pronounced and deep like a canyon. The priest had also brought coffee and hot chocolate for Martín. I could smell the steaming chocolate, so rich I could nearly taste it from across the table. Father Gabriel introduced me as a doctor and a friend of Germán.

"Reconciliation begins here," the priest announced.

"You're a doctor?" Martín asked.

"Well, nearly so. By the end of the year."

"A medical doctor?" he asked, with confusion or hope in his eyes.

"A different kind of doctor," I corrected him. "One that studies man and cultures."

"And what do you find here, doctor?" he asked.

"I find a town that needs healing." He asked about Hortencia.

"She will be okay," I assured him. "She is healing physically."

"What other way is there?" I stared at him for a moment. I could see the nervousness in his eyes, uneasiness and fear. And he looked like he could lie down and sleep for a long time, perhaps through a harvest or more.

"The spirit will also need time to heal," I said.

Father Gabriel interjected, "with God's help and our prayers."

"I would like to hear your story, Martín," I said. "I'd like to understand how you've survived these months and how you made your way back to La Purísima."

He spoke, almost in reflex. "I will tell you doctor, for Father Gabriel and for my brother, Benito. My story is really his story," he said respectfully. "It's my brother's story."

Father Gabriel sat next to Martín and with his eyes or some simple gesture urged Martín to speak. Martín looked down at the steaming cup of chocolate and wrapped his sinewy hands around the cup, as if finding security and strength.

"It was over a year ago," he began. "It was my first time to cross. The others had gone before. We were four: Jesús, Germán, Benito and I. Jesús was the oldest and I was the youngest—just twenty-one then. I thought we should hire a coyote once we got to the border, you know, to help us cross. Well, the others didn't think the same, especially Germán. He kind of became the leader. He just took charge and the rest of us followed him, like cattle I guess. We followed him like stupid cattle. When we finally reached the Río Bravo, after two or three days,

I don't remember, Germán told us he knew where to cross. An easy place where any man could get across. It was isolated and safe from *la migra*. I believed him. We all did. There was no reason not to, he had done it before."

"Who went first?" Father Gabriel asked.

"Germán."

"How was the river that day?" I asked.

"The river didn't seem deep. Germán began to cross and the water didn't reach his waist. The current ran steadily, but not too fast, I thought. But when I replayed it later I saw it differently. I saw that the water's current was swift and swirled dangerously in places. We never should have tried." I asked Martín if he was afraid.

He instantly replied, "no." Then there was a pause. "Yes," he changed his answer. "I was afraid. It doesn't matter now," he said looking straight at me. He was tired of hiding. "I had to follow. I was the youngest. The crossing is a mark of manhood," he said. "I didn't have a choice." Martín fidgeted in his chair, uneasy, a look of shame washed over him.

"And after Germán crossed?" Father Martín asked.

"Jesús went next and crossed safely. I was becoming more nervous and fearful then. A strange, negative voice kept running through my mind. 'You won't make it', it said. I had never heard the voice before. Over and over it echoed in my head. 'You won't make it'. I don't know where it came from. Inside me somewhere I suppose. There was no one else." Martín looked off into the room's darkness before speaking again.

"And then my brother was in the river and slowly making his way while that evil voice drummed in my head." Martín quieted and took a sip from the hot chocolate. The deep hollow in his throat moved. His eyes looked watery, but it may just have been the reflection from the lamp. Outside the church the storm was upon us, rolling thunder from the earth's bowels echoed through La Purísima and seemed to shake the unsteady structure around us.

"Go on son," Father Gabriel urged.

"And then the bank broke," Martín said coldly. "It just crumbled, fell apart in an instant, and the water surged and lifted Benito from his feet. It happened so fast. There was nothing I could do. In a flash my brother was washed away. He was gone. I ran along the bank as fast and hard as I could as my eyes searched the water. But it was no use. There was nothing left of him. That voice in my head had stopped and I could faintly hear Germán calling me. 'He's gone!' He called from across the river. He waved me back upstream. You can cross further up, he shouted, as if my brother's death meant nothing. He didn't even blink and I hate him for that! He led Benito to his death and then he didn't even care. Like Benito was nothing. He was my brother!"

Martín's voice was raised now and intensity consumed his face and eyes, and what I thought were tears earlier, now I could see clearly falling from his eyes. It pained him to relive that day.

"Wasn't Germán just serving the role of the leader – to keep going and to get you safely across? Maybe that was all it was," I said.

"He didn't care," Martín said defiantly. "I ran back to a place upstream from where the river bank had collapsed. Germán told me to cross. He insisted. But the more he did the angrier I became. He shouted to me. 'There is nothing else! Come!' But I stood like a tree, frozen by anguish and fear. My brother was dead." Martín slumped in the chair.

"I hated everything just then. Especially La Purísima and the passage – that forced passage that none of us has a choice about. I wanted to stay and do what little I could here. I turned my back on the river and when I did I turned away from La Purísima forever. I knew if I didn't cross I could never openly return to this place. There is shame in turning back, doctor. Maybe Benito has it better. He's dead, but not a coward."

Martín was tense now. His upper body leaned uncomfortably onto the table. He moved impulsively and jerkily. His eyes looked ahead, not at either of us, not at anything, just a blank and distant stare. He spoke again.

"And the last thing I looked at before turning was Germán's uncaring face, the one that had led us here to this end. He continued to call for me to cross. Germán's voice was that of the whole town, all of La Purísima begging me to do what every other man had done or would do. My manhood required it. Only a coward would turn away." Martín's eyes grew moist again.

Father Gabriel said softly, "what next son?"

The rain had eased up now, just a dull patter on the stone parish. Martín's body suddenly went limp and slumped in the chair. All of the rigidity escaped his body. He had surrendered, it seemed, to a calmer force. Something other than hate and anger embraced him now. He let go.

"I ran," he said softly, almost with a laugh and a surrendering admission, like it didn't matter anymore. "I turned and ran as fast as I could back into Mexico. Like a coward, I'd never be a man now."

"Where were you running?" Father Gabriel asked.

"I don't know," he said.

"Toward home?"

"Away, doctor," he answered. "I was running away from the crossing, from Germán, and La Purísima. I suppose I ran for my life. Now I wonder if I ran from my life, because I can't go back now."

Martín seemed more like a victim now, a casualty like his brother. The rain had stopped and the night was still again. It was silent and remote beyond the window of the room. The lamp burned in all three of us now, in our eyes, and somewhere deep in each of us.

Martín had struggled against the desert, stumbling and breaking earth and rock in his path. He grew delirious and was conscious only of the horizon swaying and shifting before him. It refused to stay still. It was just Martín and the desert. He ran until nightfall. When he finally stopped he realized his wounds. He had cuts from cactus needles and rock.

"But they were nothing compared to what I felt inside. There was a terrible wound inside. I cried for Benito that night," Martín admitted. "I went to sleep with it and woke up with it for two nights. The desert. I never want to see it again," he said with certainty. "The desert only increased my hate for Germán and La Purísima."

"When did you think of revenge?" I asked him.

"I thought of it then, but I didn't know how. Revenge would have to wait. I wandered the desert for two days before finding a highway," Martín explained as he gazed into the reassuring face of Father Gabriel. He looked deeply at the priest. "During the day the desert is orange and red, then when the sun lowers it changes to purple, a violet color, almost beautiful if it weren't so desolate and dry. What a strange place. I don't know how any life survives there, Father," he said with awe and amazement in his voice. "But it does: plants, lizards, birds...somehow life survives." He paused.

"I made it to a highway completely by chance and staggered, maybe in circles. It was nothing but luck."

"There is no such thing as luck, Martín. It is fate," the priest said to him.

"I thought I was dying. Two men in a pickup truck found me and gave me water and I lay down in the flatbed. I slept all the way to Torreón. The two men woke me when we arrived and I was left in the center of Torreón. I never thanked them, but they saved my life. I had nowhere to go and didn't know the city. I had never before left the state of Michoacán."

"What about money?" the priest asked.

"I had little, maybe three thousand pesos," he recalled. "No more than that. I remember that first night I slept in the street, coiled up in a fist. I shivered all night. Maybe it was the cold, but all the next day and evening I thought of the company of a woman. Any woman, it didn't matter then. Forgive me, Father. I was weak and I used some of the little money I had. I paid for an hour; it was very cheap. She must have felt sorry for me because she let me stay with her the whole night. She had a room, like a closet really, with a blue cloth that worked like a door for privacy. That night was filled with voices and sounds I'd never heard before. If not for her, I would have been afraid."

Martín seemed lost now, reliving those moments.

"All I remember is that night went so quickly, not

even half of a night spent in the desert. I stayed several days in Torreón until I had my strength back. That girl wanted me to stay with her or to come along with me. She wanted to leave her life. That's what I learned most on my return. Many people want to leave their lives. I told her there was no place for her with a coward. She cried a little and then we parted."

"Were you planning to return to La Purísima?" I asked him.

"Not here, not this town, but to Michoacán. It was all I knew. I couldn't even imagine another place. Of course, I needed to get word to my family about Benito. It was over a month before I arrived in Morelia."

"Where did you stay along the way?" Father Gabriel asked him.

"Different places, with people I met or on the street. I slept in a mission a couple nights, Father. In Fresnillo, but I think it was Franciscan," he said apologetically. "I spent time in Zacatecas, Aguascalientes, and Guanajuato, always moving south, and when I reached Salamanca I finally found the courage to write a letter to my mother. I told her about Benito. I didn't have the courage to go home though and in a sense she lost two sons that day in the river. God knows she has suffered," he said with sadness.

"I have spoken to her. At least she knows you're alive, Martín. She has peace in that," Father Gabriel said. Martín went on.

"I learned later that Father Gabriel held a Mass for Benito and that there is a grave out back of the parish. Well, it's empty, but what choice do we have?"

"We held out hope that you might appear that day,

Martín," Father Gabriel recalled. Martín shook his head.

"I never could have. Not even for Benito," he admitted.

"There will be another Mass for your brother next week," Father Gabriel said. "Your mother asked for one in his memory every year on July fifth, his birthday. Maybe you will be there for this one," Father Gabriel said hopefully.

Martín responded with uncertainty in his voice. "I don't know, Father." His voice seemed far off now, like his mind was used up with memory and he had no more space for present or future thoughts.

"After sending the letter I stayed near Lake Cuitzeo for a few days before coming to Morelia. But when I arrived in Morelia I knew I couldn't stay. The mountain peaks around the city stared and all I thought of was the open and the fields. I couldn't stand the noise of the city. I couldn't survive there. And so I went to the sierra. The one with the thousand peaks. The ones that look down on La Purísima. From up there the town is only a speck when you look down at it. Just a cut out piece of concrete," he said sadly. "It is nothing. You can see the Carácuaro running along side of the town, right along the parish grounds here," he said as he kind of opened up his shoulder toward the back of the church.

"I spent the first weeks in a tiny cave. I couldn't stand upright it was so small. There are many caves here in the hills. Then I met up with some marijuana growers. I stayed with them for many weeks, helping them grow and harvest. They never asked questions. They fed me and let me stay in their camps. For a while I forgot about everything, about Germán and La Purísima. But that didn't last," Martín admitted.

He learned he couldn't run, at least not forever.

"I was still a coward and I hated Germán for killing my brother," he said.

"But Germán didn't kill him," I said.

"Well, he might as well have," Martín shot back. "He led us across the river where he did."

"But it was the river that killed your brother, a random act of nature." I tried to convince him. "It was an accident," I said, perhaps out of place.

"But you don't understand, doctor. I can't blame the river. How can you hate the river or nature? You need a man to hate," he said.

His words made me feel cold and rigid. Martín began again and it seemed like if he stopped talking he wouldn't be able to start again. He needed to release it in one long stream.

"I thought of revenge again and I set out on my own. I set up my own camp and began to plan an act of revenge against Germán, Jesús – the entire town." He paused and drew some deep breaths. "But now I'm sorry. It has solved nothing," he confessed.

"Is that when you came to me, Martín?" Father Gabriel asked.

"It was then when I wrestled with the idea of revenge. I came down secretly from the sierra one night to La Purísima. It didn't feel like my home anymore. My home was the mountains. Father Gabriel was writing at this very table," he said, "while the rest of the town slept. It was right after the men had gone north again."

Martín admitted how he struggled with everything then.

"My brother's death, the family I had abandoned, and that burning hate inside me. Father Gabriel pleaded with me for peace, to let it go. God would heal my wounds." The priest reached over, attempting to take Martín's hand, but he drew back. "But hate is strong," Martín said callously.

Martín's hate seemed only to grow stronger with the passing months, eating away at him. He wanted to hurt Germán, and Hortencia seemed the best way to do it.

"It was the easiest and most vicious way too," he confessed with shame.

"Hate is a terrible thing," Father Gabriel professed. "A blinding thing."

"It's strange how something inside me didn't want revenge. It just wanted to go home, back to the way things were when Benito was alive. That's why I came here to see Father Gabriel. Because of that small part of me that felt different," Martín said. "I guess I was hoping that in some miraculous act or change of heart, I could let it all go. You know, just forget it all."

Martín rubbed his tired eyes and ran his fingers through his now dry hair. The night had almost passed and soon it would begin to get light. I knew that before the new dawn broke Martín would be gone. He would return to the sierra and to his hidden cove in tucked away seclusion.

"There are no miracles," I said. "Only surprises and sometimes happy endings."

"Hate won," he admitted. "And bitterness. Do you understand now, doctor? That's why I lashed out at Hortencia and went to her bed that night. My intent was to violate her, but she fought back harder and stronger than I thought. Then I just struck her several times and ran."

"What about Jesús?" I asked.

"It was hate again. I went to his home only to find that his family was gone. As I was leaving the dog trotted after me, friendly and gentle, just the same as La Purísima seems on the surface. But it's not. It pushes you away to a strange land. You go or you die trying. I hit the dog and he went quiet. This town may have to change its name," Martín said as he turned to the priest. He eased out of the chair, his clothes nearly dry.

"Why change the name?" Father Gabriel asked.

"It isn't pure," he said coldly. "Maybe it never was pure. But for sure it isn't now."

Martín needed to go. The new day was dawning. He had spent the night reciting his story or confessing it. I thanked him for meeting us and he was gone.

XIII

I stayed with Father Gabriel until mid-morning, when the sun had risen above the eucalyptus tree outside his window. It was Sunday and he asked me to stay for the Mass. I couldn't.

"I have things to do and besides that's for the faithful."

I returned to the cyber-café in search of a message from Jennifer. I found one. It was angry and hurtful. Why hadn't I called? Why hadn't she heard from me? Just a terse, cryptic message, is that all she was worth? She doubted the wedding now. She doubted everything that I was. What are you chasing in Mexico? I was nearly too tired to care, yet I must have because I went directly to the pharmacy to phone her. She was home and repeated the same words that were written in the message.

"I'm tired," I told her. "I've been up all night."

"I've been up every night since you left," she snarled, "waiting and worrying. Is this how it is?"

"What do you mean?"

"Is this what fieldwork is all about? I never hear from you! I can't live like that!" she cried.

"This isn't exactly field work," I told her.

"Then what do you call it, vacation?"

I suppose she had reason to be angry. After all, I hadn't spoken to her since I arrived over a week ago. But I had tried to call her at work that day.

"I don't know anymore, Paul," she admitted. "I don't know if this will really work. Your profession and all..." Her words trailed off.

At first I wanted to disagree with her and convince her that everything would be fine. I would be home in a day or two and we would work it all out. I'm sure I could have found the right comforting words—the ones she secretly begged for. But I never found them. I didn't even try to find them.

"I don't know either, Jen. Maybe our lives and our professions are just too different." That was it and we hung up.

There would be more discussion between us, but the truth was, I really didn't care. Maybe it was the lack of sleep or the long night with Martín, but I felt a sense of indifference now. It was the same thing that I had found in so many Mexican eyes: that vacant, remote look of insolence from eyes that forever turn away. I wondered if it was in my own eyes now. Had it replaced whatever had been there before? I didn't even know what had been there before. What preceded the insolence? I wondered the same for Mexico. Had it been the Conquest, the forced conversion to Christianity, or the Revolution that lives on only in rhetoric? So much violence and struggle had washed clean away whatever loomed in those eyes before—in the eyes of the indigenous.

I was tired and still had the long walk back to the house. As I passed an elementary school on my way out of town I noticed a long queue of people. It was election day. I had forgotten. Change was in the air, the shifting, and sinuous thread of change. But possibly not for La Purísima- not here. Nothing ever changes here. Only the timeless pace of boredom and monotony was here, drowsy and uncaring. The pure see no reason for change.

I walked along the main road in broad daylight under the heat of the early July sun. I was in the open, and exposed, hugging neither tree line nor river, just the open air, stagnant and thick. When I arrived at the house I went immediately to my room and sifted through my duffel bag. The silver earrings I had bought for Jennifer were there. On the patio I found Lilia soaking the sun.

"I have something for you," I said.

"For me?" She was surprised and maybe embarrassed. I handed her the earrings.

"Thank you," she said. "But what for?"

"No reason," I told her. "They're for you." She thanked me with a confused, but happy look on her face and I wandered back to the room and fell asleep.

I slept until mid-afternoon. I woke to the smell of dinner and I found Lilia, her grandfather, and her parents in the kitchen. There were beans; there were always beans. Beans are the staple of Mexico, especially for the poor. Lilia was wearing the earrings I had given her.

"There is news of change," Lilia's father announced.

"There is rumor that the people will vote out the PRI. I never thought I would live to see it."

"Who knows what that will mean?" Lilia's mother mused. "For us, nothing I suppose."

Then Lilia piped in cynically. "One is the same as the other to me."

My father had taught me that two subjects to avoid in conversation were religion and politics. I broke that rule often.

"Who was your candidate?" I asked Lilia's grandfather, who was mopping up beans with a shred of tortilla.

"Mine?" He looked up, surprised anyone would ask his opinion. "Well, son, my candidate is gone," he answered soberly.

"Gone where?" I asked.

"Only God knows. He's dead," he informed me. "He's been dead since 1970. Lázaro Cárdenas is the only candidate for the people." Cárdenas had been a reformist governor here in Michoacán back in the 1930s and later president of the Republic.

After dinner I sat on the patio. Lilia came out after siesta and we walked to the river. The river was high from the night's rain. We crossed the shaky bridge and strolled toward the black mountains in the distance. Never had I known a world so green.

"Will you leave soon?" she asked.

Without thinking I responded, "in a few days I suspect. Once Germán returns."

"Do you think he will find Martín?" she asked.

"I don't know. The mountains are so dense and vast. What do you think, Lilia?" Lilia slowed her pace and we settled near a cluster of trees where the sun couldn't reach us.

"I don't think he needs to look," she said. "Martín will eventually come back. A man never leaves his home, at least not for good."

Lilia meant physically never leave it and in Mexico that might be true. The country is strongly bound by family and by region. But I thought it might be true of men in all places. Physically yes, a man can move and put geography between himself and his birthplace. But in his heart he never truly leaves it. It is forever in him. What I have learned is that one place is the same as another.

"Will you ever return here?" she asked.

"Perhaps," I answered, not knowing, not thinking a day into the future.

Lilia was looking at me now and the earrings I had given her were swaying, reflecting the afternoon light. Her eyes were big and beautiful, such a mystery. We gazed at each other for a long time. I thought of how different she would be if she had left her home and pursued her dream. I sensed a trace of bitterness in Lilia for not having pursued it. She had the excuse of the family and how she was needed here. Is it fair for a family to put out the simple dream of its only daughter, like drowning a match that is desperate to light? Perhaps it had taken her will. Who can say what is best? I was simply an objective observer.

"You are different," she said.

"In what way?"

"In every way."

We were standing close together now. I searched her black eyes. I carefully lifted my hand and touched one of the smooth, silver earrings and Lilia dropped her head to one side in embarrassment, or from the tickle. I caressed her neck and admired her bare, copper colored shoulders. Our lips came together, for a moment, or for a long time, I couldn't say. Her mouth was cool and I found her scent free of perfumes and lotions. Curiously, Lilia was absent of artificial odors. All I could find was the scent of soft and sun drenched skin. If she were a flower she would certainly be a begonia. We sat together in the short grass and watched the smoky sky drift through the mountain peaks. We sat next to a cluster of trees surrounded by cornfields, a wall of gold silk tassels in every direction. With my arm cradled around her shoulder we passed the afternoon.

Before long we rose and returned to the house. We found Salvador speaking with Lilia's father. He was looking for Germán and was visibly shaken to learn that he hadn't returned. He wanted to set out on his own and search for Germán.

"I'll go to the sierra. I know them well," he said, trying to convince us.

"No," I cut in insistently. "Germán will return soon. Give him another day or two." It took all of us to convince Salvador to stay and watch the house and care for Magnolia.

"I wish Martín did come back," he said angrily. "I'd fix him for good, so he'd never hurt anyone again!"

Salvador was out of himself it seemed, ranting and pacing the room. His eyes were sharp and greenish, and he made me think of the onyx jaguar in my room back in Chicago. They had the same eyes, but the man's were less cunning, less sleek, just raw strength and with the harsh honesty of a child. He breathed heavily and it required all of us to console him. It required more than strength, but also words. Lilia understood him best and spoke to him tenderly, in simple words that he could understand. He eventually calmed and sat on the floor in the corner of the room and clutched his legs to his chest and rocked.

"Don't tell Magnolia," he pleaded. "Don't tell Magnolia. She'd be angry I made a scene." Salvador apologized and everyone but Lilia left the room. We all sneaked out as if we had just comforted a wailing infant, careful not to wake him during our exit.

The sun was setting now and the sky was a swirl of orange and magenta over the black mountains. I wanted out of here now. I was ready to go home. But I couldn't leave until Germán returned and something was settled with Martín. I felt part of this now and I knew that the gray line of profession had dissolved.

XIV

The next morning I wandered out to the back patio. Sitting in a plastic chair facing the mountains was Germán. He had returned in the night. His shoulders slumped and dejection and failure were written all over his weary body. I approached slowly and cautiously like one would a strange animal in the wild. In some way I felt I had betrayed him. After all, I had met with the man he had searched for in the dense hills for days now. He was ravaged by the search. His clothes were torn and when I came around to look at his face I saw that he was thinner and his black, watery eyes had dried and all hope seemed lost in the ocular drought.

Germán looked at me, dead like, as if the sierra had stolen everything from him. I knew he hadn't found Martín.

"Any trace?" I asked.

"A lead or two is all," he said. His voice was rough. "I met some men in the sierra who believe they had seen him a month or more ago. But nothing more than that.

He knows the mountains by now and how to survive in them. He won't be found unless he wants to. I'm convinced of that now."

I took another of the chairs and sat next to him. A *cenzontle* bird cried loudly from its perch on one of the patio's sun swept walls. The dull colored wall was chipped and cracking, the color of nothing.

"Sometimes I wonder why I care about this town," he said.

"It's your home," I reminded him.

"Up there," he motioned toward the sierra; "this town is nothing. It's just one of many little specks at the base of the mountain – nothing more than that. One of the nights when I was in the mountains I sat and looked down at La Purísima. I could see the parish and the dead streets around it, just crumbling strips of stone. That's when I realized La Purísima is nothing." He seemed angry now. I had heard the same negating words from Martín.

"That's just disappointment talking," I told him.

"Perhaps," he said and went on. "I continued to look over the town as it grew dark. When it was completely dark I noticed one dim light in the town. It was at the church. One lonely light burned all night."

I wondered if that was the night that the three of us met at the parish.

"Did it storm that night?" I asked him.

He looked curious. "It did. Not long after dark a strong storm came and I took cover. Why?" he asked. I paused, not sure whether to tell him about the meeting. Though I knew I had to.

"I was at the church that night. Two nights ago," I said.

"With Father Gabriel?"

"Yes."

"What for? What happened?" His eyes grew large and I'm sure he feared Martín had struck again.

"Hortencia?" he asked urgently and shot up from the chair.

"No, it's not Hortencia. She's fine," I assured him. "I met with Father Gabriel and Martín." I just blurted it out. "He came down from the sierra that night you saw the light. He agreed to meet with the priest and me at the parish."

Germán's face washed over with a blank, disbelieving stare. He looked as if the wind had been sucked from his lungs.

"You saw Martín?" he asked in a slow stammer. "You talked to him?" he asked, frantically pacing the patio searching the pavement at his feet, like looking for a lost diamond or other precious gem. "Why didn't you...?" he began. "You let him go? *Maestro*, how could you?"

There was anger in his eyes now, a fierce, raw anger. And likely more was disappointment.

"Had you been here it would have been different," I told him. "Martín wants peace now. Father Gabriel has convinced him that letting go is all that is left. To let go of Benito and loosen his grip on the hate that consumes him."

"What about my hate?" Germán shouted. "What about Martín paying for what he did to Hortencia?"

"Father Gabriel is seeking reconciliation," I told him. "For you, Martín, and more importantly for all of La Purísima. Martín doesn't blame you anymore," I said, perhaps stretching the truth. "He blames this town and the passage north – not one man."

Our voices had steadily grown louder. Lilia came out onto the patio. Her wide eyes looked at Germán and she saw the madness in his weary face.

"What is it, brother?" she asked, fearful of what she saw. Germán shielded her, protecting her he thought, as men sometimes feign to do.

"Nothing, Lilia." But that response was only a cry for her to pursue.

"Of course it's something!"

"Doesn't she have a right to know?" I cut in. "Martín has come back," I said. "And I've met with him." Lilia drew closer.

"A man always comes home," she said as if she already knew.

"He wants peace now," I said. "Father Gabriel wants a meeting with Germán and Martín – to save La Purísima. To put all of this behind," I told them. Lilia absorbed the words.

"I don't know how," Germán said more calmly now, as if resignation was taking hold. "Martín can't be in this town, not after what he did to Hortencia. I can't let that happen. I won't let that happen!"

"Something can be agreed upon," I tried to convince him. "An agreement where everyone can survive, even this town."

Then Lilia spoke. "Maybe he's right. Father Gabriel

might have a solution, one that you and Martín can agree upon. You have to try," she begged her brother. "The whole town is afraid and angry. What good is there in that?"

"There's no good in that. None at all. But the town's grief is not my fault. I didn't kill Benito. And I'll tell Father Gabriel that God killed him and then we'll see who's angry. How will the almighty priest respond? Father Gabriel will have to answer for God. He can answer why Benito died!"

"I told Martín why Benito died," I said. "It was simply an accident. No man can answer to that. Nature killed him. The unpredictable ebb and flow of the river and the force of the current." Lilia joined forces with me and began to persuade Germán.

"At least agree to talk, Germán. Please. You know how mother has always taught us civility. Well, this is your chance. Sit down with the men," she pleaded with him. "Our family is better than that, Germán."

"Martín shouldn't have the same rights I do," Germán said, looking away from us. "I'm reduced to what he is. He gave those rights away when he slipped into Hortencia's room."

"Every man has the right to talk," I told him. "To sit down in good faith."

At long last Germán agreed. I had witnessed something innate, such strength and humility. It went beyond economics, surpassed politics and social strata too. It was in the man and in the woman, embedded inside somehow. Germán simply wanted to see Hortencia again. I don't think he cared so much about the town. If it was saved in the process, then so be it. But the truth was he wanted Hortencia back. In the eyes of her family he wanted to return as a good and honest man.

"If a meeting with the priest will get me back to Hortencia, I'll do it," Germán said. "I'll do anything now for that chance."

Maybe our efforts, Lilia's and mine, convinced him. Or perhaps he was tired and had already surrendered to the sierra and its thousand peaks. It didn't matter, he had agreed to meet with Martín and Father Gabriel. Germán wanted to go immediately.

"If we're going to do this," he said, "let's do it now."

Father Gabriel was waiting for us. He knew Germán was back and that we would come quickly to the parish. As he had told me, he knew things before they happened. He had eyes and ears in the community, little ones I assumed, no more than belt high. The little spies were the children who scurried about town, their little black heads, like suede, seen only in flashes as their stick legs dashed between dark doorways and shadow strewn streets. They were wrapped only in white cotton drawers or draped in white sheets with leather sandals on their feet.

When I looked at them and into their liquid eyes I felt something like sympathy. Sympathy, for their fathers were gone half the year or more in the United States. I hoped things changed before they came of age and that the passage into manhood would be different. Perhaps then there would be no more Benitos and Martíns. No more empty graves behind the parish, and no more ghosts drifting in the sierra, haunting La Purísima or any other town. Economics can be cruel. Perhaps there would be change and with it some level of prosperity for rural Mexico.

We spoke with Father Gabriel in his familiar room in the church. He wasn't surprised to see Germán. Germán rarely looked at him, keeping his eyes glued to the floor. Perhaps they had searched too much over the past days and were weary from scanning valley and mountain. Germán had looked into so many desperate faces. He had stared into faces in the streets of Pátzcuaro and into the faces of the peripheral people surviving in the sierra.

"I'll send the boy this evening," Father Gabriel told us. "Tomorrow night we meet here after dark."

XV

It was July fourth, Independence Day back home. Of course, there were no fireworks or celebrations and the day moved slowly. It was a hot, sticky day, no different from many of the others. Lilia and her parents had crawled to the sun's reach out front and I sat on the back patio. Germán still slept. I watched the shadows of a hibiscus bush spattered on the patio floor, surrounded in a pink hue from the morning light. There was a rustle of grass out back and I tensed for a moment in uncertainty.

Around the edge of the field came Salvador, bounding along without a breath of finesse. He had heard Germán was back. News here traveled through invisible channels.

"He's asleep," I informed him. He stood beside me, willing to wait as long as it took, breathing heavily over me. He was as impatient as a child was. It wasn't long though when Germán stepped into the glaring sun.

"Did you find him?" Salvador asked immediately. Germán scratched his head.

"No, he found me," he answered impulsively and irritably. Salvador looked more confused now and kind of glared at Germán, vacant like.

"There's a meeting tonight at the parish," Germán told him.

"With Martín?"

Germán told him it was true. "This will be settled once and for all."

"How can it be settled at the church? I don't understand..."

"Nobody understands," Germán said. "Nobody understands anything, but we'll go anyway. Some things can't be explained." Germán told Salvador to go. "Stay with Magnolia. That's what you should do now." Salvador reluctantly walked off.

"And keep your mouth shut about what I told you." Salvador turned back. He looked like a hurt child. He would never disobey Germán. "Now go," Germán said, and he did.

The afternoon dragged more slowly than the morning. It trudged along like it didn't want to get there, like it never would get dark. The air grew more stagnant as the day progressed, no breeze, just the infinite weight of boredom and waiting. This place was always waiting —waiting for Death to come snatch it. In a sense, we all are, but to dwell on it and let it consume us like a disease only suspends Life. The whole town was stalled, indefinitely frozen in its own quagmire of superstitions and ghosts.

Death hung over this place like the mountains and the black, liquid nights. The only light burned dimly through the parish window where a young priest wrote letters. While around the parish, not in the empty lingering streets, but within the homes, people slept or fingered rosaries, pulled covers up to their necks, or better, over their heads to ward off Death. The ignominy of La Purísima sickened me. People hid behind thick doors, in shadowy stairwells, or in dark doorways peeking, searching for Death and scheming of ways to fend it off or defeat it. In the end, we will all be called to embrace it. There is nothing else.

And now there was more waiting. Waiting for the night sky to come when the black mountains will become one with it. In the night, ghosts consume La Purísima and only Death walks the lonely streets. The river runs slower, more deliberate now to allow the ghosts a drink – it is the salvation of the river. For its own survival, it allows the ghosts to drink from its body. The only way the river knows how to ward off Death is to cut a deal. Befriend it, don't offend it.

In the still, limpid night we walked. The river's gentle rush was our sole guide. The virgin night disturbed only by the two of us passing along the Carácuaro's banks and Martín carefully descending from the sierra. The parish's burning lamp was our beacon. And Father Gabriel waiting and writing letters as the night progressed. Writing to ghosts or gods, pleading for the salvation of La Purísima and all of its desperate souls. The souls, most of whom were never seen, but they existed. The fear of revenge, of Martín lurking, kept them cloaked in the shadows. The fear would end tonight. Perhaps tomorrow things would be different. Perhaps

La Purísima would rise from the weight of fear and the river would wash superstition and the looming nightmare of another attack away.

We came upon the parish. The lamp burned inside. Father Gabriel and Martín sat next to one another at the table. The father's writing had been set aside. He was not wearing the collar. Perhaps he wanted less space between us and to say that we are all men. No cloth separates us, and he, like us, was nothing more than an ordinary man.

Martín refused to look up and glued his eyes, orange from the lamp, to the table and the stack of writing. Perhaps he refused out of shame, guilt, or else fear of the hate and rage inside him. But the truth was he was letting go, releasing that cancerous hate inside him. I had seen it, only a glimmer, but I had seen it beginning to fade.

Germán and I walked into the room. Germán looked weary, still not recovered from his days in the sierra. When he saw Martín his face changed. It went from wary, to serious and intense. His eyes darted near Martín and then drove into him as we moved toward the center of the room. We sat across from Martín. Father Gabriel was seated next to him in a show of support. The priest thanked the two men for their courage. Father Gabriel thanked me too and for a moment I felt awkward, like I didn't belong. Or else I felt awkward because I was part of it now and something more than an observer.

Martín took the first sober steps. "I'm sorry for what I did to Hortencia."

"If you wanted me, you should have come looking," Germán said. "Getting to me through her was weak and cowardly."

Father Gabriel stepped in. "But he is sorry now. God has already forgiven him and that is what really matters." Martín lifted his eyes.

"Has God forgiven you?" he asked, his eyes glued to Germán.

"I don't need God's forgiveness," Germán replied. "I've given up on Him. Besides, there's nothing to forgive."

"There's my brother!" Martín cried.

"But that's where you are mistaken. I didn't kill your brother. God did," Germán said.

"You blame God for what happened on the river?" Martín asked.

"He let it happen, didn't He?" Germán asked. There was no response. Germán continued. "I rejected God that day because of Benito's death and because you ran scared. I thought you might be dead too. I rejected God because of you!"

"God never left and he wants you back." Father Gabriel gently spoke the words of his profession.

"I don't care anymore," Germán said bitterly. "I'm tired and I don't care."

I had been quiet, but something told me to speak. Something made me act and my mouth moved.

"I think the important lesson is to acknowledge Benito's death as an accident. That is truly what it was— nothing more than a terrible accident. It happened and has touched and changed many lives. But until both of you accept that it was an accident, there will be no peace in La Purísima."

Father Gabriel looked at me and I thought he would be angry for pushing God aside. But he wasn't and he surprised me with what he said.

"Paul is right. Looking for a man to blame will only breed hate. No man is guilty here."

"You're wrong, Father. Martín is guilty," Germán said. "He's guilty for what he did to Hortencia. That is no mistake."

"He has apologized," Father Gabriel reminded him.

"I can't let that stand," Germán said. "Martín cannot live in La Purísima. He can no longer be one of us. He doesn't have the right."

"I don't want to come back," Martín admitted. "I only came back for revenge and that was a mistake. Nothing has changed and Benito is gone for good."

"But son," Father Gabriel started, "you can't live in the mountains. That is no life for a man."

"No, I'll go away for good. To a place that won't force me to go north. I'll go south to Guerrero or back north to Fresnillo or Torreón. I know other places now."

"That is the only solution," Germán said. "You must go away forever. And to think if I had found you in the sierra I would have killed you on the spot, without hesitation. Go away and never come back," Germán said coldly. "And for that, I will get my Hortencia back. And this town can have peace again, whatever that is worth."

Martín's head hung low. It seemed he was thinking about the fact he would never come back to his home. Yet he understood that there was no other solution.

"Tomorrow would be Benito's birthday," Father Gabriel said. "We are having a Mass. Martín, I would like you to be there. To remember Benito and pay respects before you go." He looked at each of us, parking his eyes for a few moments. "I want all of us to be there to show the town that we've reconciled. La Purísima can celebrate."

"I don't know," Germán said. "How can I be there with Martín after what has happened?"

"After tomorrow, Martín will be gone," Father Gabriel said. "A show of reconciliation and forgiveness will heal the town. It's for the greater good. Both of your attendance will send a message of hope to the community." Germán and Martín reluctantly agreed.

The meeting was over. It had gone more quickly than I had anticipated, but the outcome was the only possibility. I thought of the Mass tomorrow. I didn't really want to go, just to stand and kneel and then march out back and stare at the ground where Benito was supposed to be. But the truth was no one knew where he was. He was dead, that was all. But I would go. It would tie the knot on my journey to La Purísima and in a sense, tomorrow would be a victory lap for the town. A time to heal and return to living. I thought of Jesús and his family, the nephews I had never met. Perhaps after I returned to Chicago there would be one last trip to Michigan to look in on them in their new life.

XVI

The events that had occurred over the past days in Mexico had nothing to do with my dissertation. The fact is they would not impact or influence my findings in any way. The results were conclusive and had been documented before I left. Yet somehow I sensed that Professor Lassene would disagree. I suppose I had learned something of Life, and of Death. I had seen the town and walked its crumbling streets, run my hands along the shadow-strewn walls and met its people. After tomorrow things would be different. Though are they ever different in thousands of towns just like La Purísima? Or is the past so vivid, so present, that it refuses to loosen its grip and release the place?

My mind drifted to the procession in Pátzcuaro. Perhaps it is only then, in festival or celebration, when people can smile and dance and forget the past and the current struggles. Only then would Lilia's bitterness be replaced by sweet tastes of festival and Germán could, for a time, truly forgive Martín for what he had done. And La Purísima as a whole could laugh at Death and mock the ghosts that ruled this place. And perhaps on the night of the festival people would sleep out from under bed covers and callused fingers would rest, leaving the rosary beads undisturbed on the bedside table. Maybe these are the things outsiders are not supposed to see.

I would likely never see this place again. Though perhaps my work would lead me to places like it in the future, places estranged from the rest of the world. Places ignored, left to their own devices and to survive by their wits and by what their parents had done before them. Or like the current generation of men, transform the way a living was made. For these men the rite of passage was redefined as a journey north. It was a harsh reminder of the serious obligation of adulthood. In the face of survival, it never ceases to amaze me what concessions will be made. It is true that economics can be cruel and will forever be the basis and the impetus for change.

It was July fifth. Benito would have been twenty-seven. I prepared my things; I would be leaving tomorrow. At the river I found Lilia washing clothes. There was a stiff breeze and the tree leaves rustled like rushing water. It sounded like ocean waves around us— a gentle and even surge against a sandy shore. Our feet stuck firmly in the muddy banks of the Carácuaro. I helped her gather the clean clothes into a basket and then we rested on nearby rocks. We watched the careless river. I had almost grown accustomed to doing what I did here in La Purísima – and that was nothing.

"When are you leaving?" Lilia asked.

"Tomorrow."

Her mouth gave a crooked smile and she fidgeted

with the cloth of her dress that gathered at her waist. She gazed at the water and then her dark eyes and thick lashes turned to me. She looked beautiful, like a portrait, with a leafy canopy overhead and the meandering river behind her. In her eyes was a kind of yearning or grasping. I believe she was leaning toward me, as if it were me she longed for. A brief gust of air or cold liquid shot through me, through my veins and insides, and I thought that I longed for that one sitting on the smooth rock across from me. It was an ache, perhaps because of the knowledge that my relationship with Jennifer was through. Or else it was simply that I longed for my home. What I knew was the feeling was misplaced.

"Do you miss your home?" she asked.

"A little. I need to return to my work."

Sadness was in her eyes, not about me leaving, but rather a sense of loss for everything that had ever come and gone in her life. The dream that she never pursued. Every dream that she had ever known seemed to be reflected in my eyes. But all that was there was a faint reflection of the meandering river, the waving current, rushing away from us, careless and burdenless.

Tomorrow I would travel and along came the doom, the stagnant, lethargic thing that burrowed deep and changed me. The hollow pit of my abdomen and the weakness, and I wondered how anyone, anywhere could be happy.

"Are you happy, Lilia?"

"I suppose," she answered unconvincingly. "I think of it, but then I resist because my choices are limited. But sometimes I think simplicity is happiness," she said. It was all she knew. I didn't tell her, but that question and concept consumes us all at one time or another.

And I could hear it murmur just below her tranquil, coppery surface.

We heard a bird's strange shriek and a sudden gust of wind came and whipped her hair and her eyelashes fluttered like two dark, mysterious butterflies. I reached over and took her hand. She squeezed me gently. It was time to get back to the house. Whatever symbols we found in each other's eyes, whatever forgotten or misplaced dreams, the sensations and longings that rose within us seemed then to vanish in the breeze, carried off into the mountains' density.

"Are you coming to the Mass this evening?" she asked as she rose from the gleaming rock. I told her I was and we began to gather the clothing.

Late that afternoon Lilia and her parents prepared for church. Her grandfather arrived too and would join us. The men slipped into their finest leather boots, stiff trousers, and broad rimmed hats. The women wore dresses and bathed heavily in perfumes. The church was crowded. I didn't realize there were so many people in all of La Purísima. They had at last escaped from their hiding places. The townspeople were drunk with pride and the women were dressed in their finest, made up gaudily with costume jewelry. The men were crowned with their finest, most elegant hats and bathed for the celebration.

We sat in a front pew; the whole family lined up with me stuck at one end like a misplaced bookend. In some way I belonged, but at the same time I didn't. Families and couples lumbered in and found seats. They looked somber and superstitiously crossed themselves as they entered and looked to the crucifix at the end of the nave.

It was ten past five and still no sign of Martín. We

had about given up on him. Father Gabriel delayed the start of the Mass as long as he could. Time meant nothing here, but a Mass was different. Reluctantly, the Mass began and there was much sitting and kneeling and genuflecting. A few of the men slept while women fanned themselves in the stifling heat. Father Gabriel spoke of peace and healing. Martín never arrived.

Afterward many parishioners trudged out to the back of the church. The grounds were nothing more than dust and stones impacted in the dry earth. Others scurried out front to the plaza where it was shaded and cooler. Those of us out back surrounded the marker and Benito's empty grave. Across from me stood the brothers' parents. They looked hollow, just two shells of people. Magnolia and Salvador were beside me. He breathed heavily and all of us sweat in the stagnant afternoon heat. Before long people began to drift away in small groups and soon only a few remained. The last were Salvador and Magnolia. They too eventually wandered off toward the plaza with the others and Germán and I were left with Father Gabriel.

"It was too difficult for Martín," Father Gabriel explained. "A man can only stand so much shame."

"As long as he's gone for good, that's all that matters," Germán said.

The altar boy rushed out of the church. His duties were finished inside and he asked for permission to go.

"Just one more thing," Father Gabriel said to him. "Will you go up the trail a little? I'd like to be sure there is no sign of Martín." The boy knew the trail and had been the liaison between the priest and the sierra. He was the priest's eyes and ears in the community. The boy dutifully scampered off toward the hills.

The three of us returned to the empty church, our steps echoed through the silence. As we gazed out at the plaza people sat along stone benches, children played, and a man selling corn popsicles pushed his cart through. Half of the plaza was in shadow and we could see the parish cupola outlined on the pavement. A flock of pigeons flew rapidly from the pavement, just a fan of gray and white, as a dog trotted toward them and then circled back to chase the children.

"The people are healing," Father Gabriel commented, rather absently. We watched the activity for some minutes and all the while I thought that Father Gabriel was right. The people are healing and returning to Life.

Just then the altar boy burst in through the back doors of the parish.

"Father!" he called, out of breath, panting like he had run the distance back. "I found him!" We turned to the boy.

"Martín," he said. "I think he's dead." His wide eyes had gone white with astonishment. Father Gabriel began to walk calmly toward the boy. The ease and calm with which he moved was a trait of his profession. The boy ignited in a run toward him, his face about to cry. Father Gabriel embraced the boy in his flowing priestly gown and wiped the tears with a handkerchief. The priest comforted the boy and calmed him.

When he quieted, Father Gabriel spoke. "Take us to him, my son."

We followed the boy out of the church and across the hard, dry earth. We descended toward the river. The priest and the boy walked hand in hand now. At the river was a man watering his horse. He wore the traditional white hat of Michoacán with a round, wide brim and a black tassel swaying in back. The river was hardly a trickle here and we could leap across without difficulty. When the man noticed the priest he instantly lowered his hat and made some apology for not attending the Mass.

"It's okay," Father Gabriel assured him. "But we need your help. Will you bring the horse and come with us?" He agreed and then returned the hat to his head. His hair, once black, was greased back and now densely streaked with white and he had the same color mustache. The man's demeanor was stiff and dry; he was known here as a local rancher. The man, hired now, and the horse took up the rear and after crossing the river we stopped at the base of the sierra. We breathed.

"How far?" Germán asked.

"Very near," the boy answered, pointing some distance up the path.

We started out. The dirt and stone trail was well defined, heavily traveled and not difficult to walk. Not one man spoke. It grew steep and treacherous further up, but we wouldn't be forced to go that far. The horse resisted, its body pitched and reared before the man regained control. He spoke to the horse and calmed the animal with long even strokes along his enormous neck. We had walked for only a short time when the boy and the priest stopped and stared off into the dense brush alongside the trail. There was hushed anticipation. Germán hurried ahead and stared with his own eyes.

"It's Martín," he said quietly. "Dead like his brother."

Instantly we knew it couldn't have been an accident. Martín was too skilled and knowledgeable of the mountains. And here it was even safe for a boy and a priest to travel. I couldn't see the body, but could feel it there in the brush up ahead under a large nopal. My stomach dropped and I thought I might be sick. My strength seemed to abandon me, and then the weakness passed and I moved to where I could see the body.

Martín's dead body was crumpled in the brush, one shoulder driven hard into the ash colored earth where he had fallen and one hand was turned back and twisted like you would never see on a breathing man. There was a clump of dried blood near his temple where flies congregated and sparred with each other. Their translucent wings assumed tints of green and pink.

"Bring the horse," Father Gabriel instructed the hired man. The priest behaved with practicality. Father Gabriel and the boy moved back down the trail to allow the rest of us to move forward. The hired man positioned the horse on the path near the body. I'd never seen a dead man before, at least one with blood still in him. Yet after the initial shock I was remarkably calm and helped move the body like anything awkward and heavy.

Germán, the hired man, and I scooped up the body. The man was making his payment, his penance for not attending the Mass. The body didn't much cooperate and nearly got away from us.

"Get his feet," Germán instructed. "I'll get him under the shoulders."

The man doing penance helped support the sagging torso. We struggled with the unruly clump, but finally conquered it and draped it crossways over the horse. Thankfully, the horse didn't resist Martín's body and we started back down the trail.

XVII

The vast Mexican sky seemed stalled and inert. The barren landscape stared up at us as we entered the churchyard, just stone scattered over dry earth and the leaning, crumbling building toward the plaza. We went along by Benito's marker. It was clear that Martín's head had been struck and the blow had killed him. Each man was silent, yet in each man's head were searching thoughts of the killer, of who might have murdered Martín. Father Gabriel may have suspected Germán, but I knew differently.

We had returned home together last night. Germán sensed the priest's suspicion or only imagined it. You couldn't guess what went through a man's mind.

"It wasn't me, Father," Germán said. "There was no reason for me to do it. We had agreed that Martín would leave. It was settled." The priest ignored him, concentrating on his duty to care for the dead.

"Now, we have to bury a man," Father Gabriel said quite matter of fact. He turned to the boy. "Fetch the burial shovel and a blanket." The boy started off, kicking up earth as he went. He ran off to the parish and quickly returned dragging a shovel and clutching a blanket.

"Father, I brought the blanket from your bed," the boy said.

"Now, go tell Martín's parents to come. They are in the plaza. And then go see *Señor* Ochoa. We'll need a good size box," Father Gabriel instructed him like a military man, one accustomed to giving orders. The boy sprinted off.

"May I dig the hole?" Germán asked. Father Gabriel handed him the shovel.

"There, next to his brother."

The sun was low on the horizon now. I turned away from its sharp, eye-level glare and watched Germán scratch at the stubborn dirt. The digging was difficult in the arid, stone riddled ground and he strained to break the earth. Small bands of people began to trickle from the sides of the parish, fanning out like ants on either side of the building. They came sluggishly, as if they were too weary to walk back behind the church, or Martín wasn't worth the effort. Some came just for the chance to see a dead man. The old women came with *rebozos* covering their heads, draping the tails around their leathery necks. The brothers' parents shuffled toward the sharp grinding sound of digging where Germán worked the obstinate earth.

"My sons, *Dios Mío*," the mother repeated. "Mother of God..." Father Gabriel assured the parents there would be a Mass later for Martín, but with the condition of the body it was best to bury him immediately.

Martín's body was laid out on a blanket. The hired man knelt beside it, fanning flies. Germán sweat heavily, dirt pasted to his cheeks. He continued to dig and about the time he finished the grave the boy had returned with *Señor* Ochoa, another man, and a simple pine box. The box was placed next to Martín's body and the three of us, the same that slumped it on the horse, lifted it into the coffin. Martín had no belongings or valuables, just a few loose coins in his pocket. We gave them to his mother who wept behind us.

Señor Ochoa had brought along a hammer and nails as he was familiar with such things, and proceeded to drive the nails after we had carefully placed the lid. We backed away and allowed Father Gabriel a few moments. He made mention of a lost son come home, brothers reunited, and some rambling about a better place. I didn't much listen to the words, except when he referred to the death as an accident. He made it sound like Martín had slipped and fallen and that the unforgiving sierra had killed him.

"And now, it doesn't matter," he said. "Martín is at peace and that is all that matters." Father Gabriel knew better, though I suppose he was protecting La Purísima from further pain and divisiveness.

"An accident," the priest told us, "not unlike his brother. It was God's will," he said as he looked empathetically at Martín's parents. I didn't understand but somehow he lied to their faces.

"The brothers are at peace and so too is La Purísima." He finished his words and then with ropes we lowered the coffin into the ground, slow and even. Germán shoveled the earth over the coffin and it was finished. How little it took to stick a man in the ground.

I never knew what Father Gabriel truly thought. I don't know if he assumed Germán had killed Martín that night after the meeting, or if he had convinced himself that it was an accident. I never spoke to Father Gabriel again. His aim had been to bring peace and reconciliation back to La Purísima, and in a sense he had accomplished that. It took a lie, a curious deception, but he had succeeded. Perhaps it was the only explanation La Purísima could tolerate.

By now it was nearly dark. Lilia and her parents had found a ride home. Germán and I chose to walk. Night fell hard. It dropped on La Purísima like a lead weight. We walked along the river, both of us silently turning over the events of the afternoon in our minds. Jesús' sister, Magnolia, and Salvador had left the plaza before Martín's body was found. We stopped at their home on the way. Magnolia was surprised by the news we brought, but felt it was for the best and that some kind of justice had been served.

"He won't bother this town anymore," she said. "Wherever he is," she predicted, "he'll get his due."

Her husband was silent, only suggesting agreement with everything she said in an adolescent nod of his head. His behavior had always been unusual, but tonight it seemed more so. I watched him closely, fidgeting, turning away, and examining the walls and floor. If I didn't know better, I would say he exhibited the mannerisms of a guilty man. He acted like a man hiding something. Then I recalled that Germán had informed Salvador about last night's meeting. Perhaps Germán had slipped, or intentionally told him in frustration or aggravation. Salvador spoke to Germán.

"It's for the best, no?" he asked, seeking Germán's approval, desperately searching his face for a sign. He sought approval from everyone, especially Germán who by now had taken Jesús' place as the male, almost father-like figure in his life.

German didn't answer right away and uncertainty was scrawled on his face. Whatever Salvador knew he realized it must remain a secret, yet he yearned for approval for what I thought now he had likely done. It seemed a logical explanation. Approval would have to come in a smile on German's face, some visible sign of pleasure or victory in Martín's death. It didn't come. Salvador became concerned, worried now that he may have done wrong.

"It's what you wanted, right?" Salvador asked nervously.

"I did," German said. "But at the meeting we had agreed Martín would go away forever. He never would have bothered us again. Maybe he didn't have to die," German admitted with reluctance.

Salvador's eyes grew large, like two full moons, and his face went pale. I could read his expression. He was like a child who is sure he has done a good deed and made his parents proud, only to learn later that he has made a complete mess of things. The child runs off to hide in disgrace, while the parents are left to wrestle with whether to praise or punish.

Approval didn't come and Salvador turned and left the room. Magnolia looked after him, but didn't budge. German looked like he had just been hit hard by something. He must have known.

"I'll talk to him," he said before stammering after Salvador. Magnolia and I stood silently for a moment and then she offered me a seat and we stumbled through conversation. I told her I was leaving tomorrow.

"Stop by on your way out of town," she said. "We'd

like to say goodbye." I would, I told her.

"And if you have anything for Jesús and the family, I can take it along," I offered. She couldn't think of anything but might by tomorrow. She gazed off into the night where Germán and Salvador had gone.

"Do you think it was an accident?" she asked. I didn't want to reveal my suspicions.

"It's possible," I told her, and I suppose it was still remotely possible. "Father Gabriel thinks so."

"Well, he is a rational man," she said. "And his opinion goes a long way in this town."

She seemed at ease with what I had said. Germán and Salvador returned to the room. Salvador's head was lowered and Germán had his arm around his neck as if pulling him along.

"What is it?" Magnolia asked sharply.

"Nothing a good night's sleep won't cure," Germán said. Magnolia stared at Salvador.

I wondered what went through his mind. Did he have a conscience? He was quiet like always, but seemed unmoved. I searched for something in his face, a sign of passion, feeling, or remorse. There was nothing but the stupefied look, the vacuous expression that was always there.

"Let's go, Paul," Germán said quietly. "It's getting late." Germán and I went back into the night.

"What did he say?" I asked.

Without a breath of hesitation, Germán answered. "He told me he killed Martín." We kept walking while Germán explained.

"Salvador hid behind the parish last night and waited for him. When Martín left, Salvador followed him a little ways up the path and then came behind and struck him in the head with an axe handle. It only took one blow. Martín went limp and never moved again. Salvador told me he did it for me, Jesús, and for all of La Purísima. He thought he had done right until I told him what happened at the parish meeting. How we had made the agreement. He killed Martín out of loyalty—simple loyalty. You can't blame a man for that. And remember, this is only half a man at that."

"What did you say to him?" I asked.

"I convinced him again that he had done right. That he had done what I wanted and Jesús would have wanted. It was the only thing, the only answer he could have tolerated."

"He thinks he has done right then?" I asked.

"No. I told him never to speak of this to anyone. Don't take pride in it. The truth is I never should have told him about the meeting last night. He doesn't have the mind for that information. He can't be blamed. I made it too easy for him."

"You can't be the blame," I told him.

"Salvador just did what I had set out to do. That's all. It's over now and we won't speak of it."

When we reached the house it was asleep. Tomorrow I would be gone.

XVIII

I slept little that night with the vision of the dead man planted in my mind and the events of the last days rolling through my head. I lay still, while Germán slept soundly on the bed nearby. Part of what had led me here was the persistent throng of the mystery of Martín. Now it had all been revealed. I thought now of getting home, of Jennifer, and closing the door on that part of my life, a part of my life that seemed so wrong now. All had become clear to me and to Jennifer over these past weeks of separation. I felt no remorse or sadness, just a vague sense of relief that we would prevent what was doomed from the start. I was tired now and was slipping off to sleep with an image of sitting with Professor Lassene, discussing the events of La Purísima. That was what I wanted most now, to sit with my mentor.

The morning left time to say goodbye. I've always believed goodbyes should be brief. Intended words that are even remotely sentimental should be scattered out at various times in the days preceding the goodbye. The final goodbye should leave nothing but the simple words, "goodbye, adios, ... adieu," and a wave of the hand. But this is never how it happens. We leave things until the end. We're that way. We postpone or procrastinate, in either case delay the final departure.

I said goodbye to Germán's parents and he and I went out front of the house. I had not seen Lilia that morning and I wondered if she hated goodbyes so much that she was hiding. Germán thanked me for coming.

"I don't know if I could have come alone, *maestro*," he admitted. "I was so sick about Hortencia." I could see him choking back, fighting his own humanity.

"She should be well now," I told him. "Go see her. The family will embrace you once again," I predicted. Germán smiled modestly.

Once Hortencia's family learned of Martín's death they again welcomed Germán into their home. They believed that he had avenged the attack on their daughter. There was a brief embrace between us, the way men do. And then I noticed Lilia emerging from behind the house, dressed plainly with an air of simple elegance.

"Next year I'll be back for the harvest," Germán said.

"I'll see you then. We're friends now," I said.

"No, *maestro*, we're *paisanos*." Germán lifted his head and turned back toward the house.

Lilia approached and I moved to greet her.

"Are you ready?" she asked.

"I am."

"Thank you for being good to my brother. He needed a friend through this."

Lilia came close to me. Her face glowed and opened

like a blooming flower. We embraced and I pressed her close to me. The embrace felt like a shoving off, a boost for a journey and a new life. As always, she was odorless. As hard as I had searched there was no distinguishing scent from her, nothing to take with me, no trace that would linger in my senses for the sake of nostalgia. Once I was home there would be nothing to invade my dreams or my lonely trips to cafés.

"I'll visit one day," I said, unthinking, just to fill the long silence.

Lilia backed away smiling. I felt something for her, affection or gratitude. It was one of those cloudy and imprecise emotions. It was what I had felt with her by the river. I suppose it was the thought of all life's possibilities and finding yourself, your image reflected in the flattering light of another's mysterious eyes. I recalled how Professor Lassene had corrected me. We don't see in others what we wish to become, but rather we see what we are. I knew I had to go. My hand rose, almost mechanically, and waved to her. I noticed she wore the earrings I had given her, the ones intended for Jennifer. They winked like stars in the morning light.

As I strode along the path toward the main road, I thought of Martín. I thought that at least he died at his home, near his birthplace, and I suppose there was some solace and comfort in that. Maybe it just made me feel better; it did little for him.

For me, I knew I would not die at home; somehow I had that knowledge. I would die in some remote, vacant place, surrounded by people I had known for only a short while. But with whom I shared camaraderie and a fondness that makes it all right and will allow me to die at peace in a strange land. The common element that transcends our differences and unites all of us is our human fragility. All of our lives possess the right to die.

Martín never wanted to make the passage north, yet his local culture demanded it. He would never be considered a man otherwise. He hated La Purísima for that and Germán became the object of that hate. After all, "you need a man to hate," Martín had told me.

My mind slipped back to my own rite of passage and to that sudden thrust into superficial manhood. It happened for me before a girl's first kiss, before a license to drive a car, and before the first bitter sip of beer. It happened for me, quite unexpectedly one day, when a grandfather's familiar goodbye kiss became a stiff handshake. I went to him to say goodbye, as always, expecting the kiss on the cheek. But instead, his hand rose in the form of a cool handshake. I lifted my own hand and clutched his and shook it. I don't know what was written on my face, but inside I can still recall the pit, my stomach dropping, and a sharp pain. Maybe that moment created the hollow place inside me, the place whose emptiness cries out on dark, silent nights and when I prepare for travel. And in those times when I sit alone at a café, push the book aside and my thoughts stray, and a bird circles the vacantness deep inside me. That day I think I learned that the world possessed cruelty. And too, that some things are required in this world, despite a powerful sting.

Martín understood the world's cruelty much better than I. All of La Purísima understood the harsh realities and the cruelty of economics. The disparity of wealth and the will to survive pulled this generation north. These men went reluctantly. And to transform economic survival into a rite of manhood made it even more difficult to turn away. It was a clever, practical deception all in the name of survival and the hope of something better one day. The punishment of choosing not to go was harsher these days. Martín knew that.

I had promised to say goodbye to Magnolia. There was no answer at the front door, so I went around to the side of the house. As I circled around something caught my eye. It was the handle of a garden hoe or pick propped against the home's gray stone. I went near it and could see it was the axe handle, the weapon Salvador must have used. The tip was gruesome. It was set in the bright sunlight, on display, no attempt made to hide or conceal the evidence. Salvador didn't think that way. I found Magnolia at the back of the house hanging wet clothes on a line.

"I'm leaving," I called to her. She turned and came toward me. "I'll look in on Jesús," I promised. She gave me the address in Michigan.

"It's his dream you know," she said. "To make a life up there. I'll never understand it," she admitted, shaking her head in disbelief. "No one could convince him differently, not even Dulce.

She went because it was his dream. But she went reluctantly."

"A man and his dream are thickly meshed," I said. "They won't part easily."

She looked off into the distance along the margins of the field. I could see a figure out there, just a black grain. It was Salvador.

"Better to have dreams I suppose," she mused. "Some of us don't even have that. We just make it from day to day and accept what little God gives us," she said, and then gazed after Salvador, at his bent, dark figure in the distance.

"We do the best we can," I said, as her thoughts drifted further to the man in the field. She didn't hear me. "I need to go now."

She turned to me again, lost in thought or worry and I left her that way. She was half-aware of me and the other was adrift along the edge of the field, gazing into nowhere.

XIX

I woke in my own bed, surrounded by my books and the other things that made me. As I inhaled the familiar scents of home the thing that most reminded me of Jennifer watched intently. The black onyx jaguar stared through the morning shadows. Its green eyes were dull, like they had lost their luster and keen perception while I was away. Or I saw them differently now. Perhaps I had changed. Jennifer would no longer fear them. Not simply because the eyes had changed, but because she would never be here again, not in the way that she once had. She and I would no longer lounge and love here, listening to those tender yet rebellious ballads of a British folk singer.

It was strange how much had changed in such a short time. My life seemed different now. We had our memories. But the truth was it really wasn't terribly different. I would wake like always, teach and study, and frequent unfamiliar cafés. The only difference was that Jennifer would no longer be in my life. I accepted that. We weren't meant for each other, as if any two people are. What was left was to say goodbye, properly. I imagined she hated me now. After all, the wedding was planned and less than six months away.

I called Jennifer at the office. We talked and agreed to meet later at a bar on Sheffield where we used to go once in awhile. It had a beer garden so we could sit outside, though we'd be interrupted intermittently when the 'L' rattled past. I just wanted it over so I didn't have to think about it anymore.

I spent the day at the university library reviewing the dissertation. As I went over it, the dry statistics and analysis, it struck me as more impersonal now. Of course it had to be. Academic papers are intended that way. I knew that the journey north, the imposed rite of passage, had an economic or material basis. But I knew names and faces now behind those trends and numbers of migrants and economic output. It was different. There were the voices and the faces of La Purísima lurking throughout the pages and the black mountains rising up, with smoky clouds drifting through them and the dense, green carpet rolling over the valley. That place was in me now. La Purísima would forever be part of me.

The bar wasn't crowded. It was a weeknight and the neighborhood team was out of town. I found a spot on an empty bench in the corner of the beer garden and leaned against the tall cedar fence behind it. A young couple sat together across the way. Their faces were burnt red and looked like they had been out here all day drinking beer. In the other direction two young women, no doubt college students, sat together. One of them was quiet while the other spoke loudly so that others could hear, like someone cared. She went to great lengths to draw attention to herself. The silent one looked either bored or drunk.

I had nearly finished my beer when Jennifer showed

up. There she was with cutoff denim shorts, a yellow tank top and sandals, every bit the all-American girl. I swallowed hard. She marched toward me as if she were reviewing a script in her mind, visibly mumbling to herself. She was tanned and shiny.

"I want this over with quickly," she said with fire in her eyes. I convinced her to sit. "You showed me your true self these past weeks," she said as she tightly folded her arms against her body. "The fact is you love your work more than you do me. As I sat home alone those nights I could see our future. It will never work."

I wasn't about to disagree. She handed me the engagement ring.

"I realized it too while I was away," I confessed. "We're too different, Jen. That's all." I could see the anger eating away, holding hostage any other feelings she might have.

"Don't you even care?" she asked. "Not even a little? You seem entirely calm about this." Even that, my acceptance, made her angry.

"I guess I've just come to terms with it," I told her. She still looked angry and I sensed her searching for words to hurt me. Anything to hurl at me, an insult... something.

"My parents hate you!" she finally blurted out, and then I noticed a tear in her eye. I felt just as bad, but it was for the best. "The wedding is off!"

I loved her at one time and maybe I still did. I don't know. This had been coming much longer than the past couple weeks. Jennifer and I were different. She straightened her legs, curved her shoulders inward, and played with a bracelet she had taken off. It was green;

the color meant something, wisdom maybe.

"Well, consider yourself free now," she said. I told her the same. "I do feel free," she admitted. "Free to go after everything I want in life."

"I'm sure you'll get it, Jen," I said, knowing just how tenacious she was. "Your ambition will take you a long way."

"What's that supposed to mean?" she asked sharply.

"Just that you have an abundance of ambition," I explained. "I just hope you can be happy and satisfied one day."

"What, ambition and happiness don't go together?" she asked.

"Well, someone once said that happiness means being free. And to be truly free you would need to let go of all ambition."

"Thanks, professor," she said sarcastically. "But you would be dead then. A person without ambition is dead!"

"Maybe that's what they meant," I said coldly.

"Maybe this is a good time for me to leave," she said.

Jennifer got up and looked at me. I gazed up at her in the twilight and I knew that a small part of me would always love her. She said goodbye and walked away. I drank another beer and then went home.

The illness that Professor Lassene wrestled with before I left for Mexico had not been a relapse of malaria after all. In fact, if treated properly with the correct antibiotics, the disease would never resurface. The professor still held on to the belief that malaria never left him. But his wife Dolores assured me it had been nothing more than a simple virus. Perhaps his untiring attempt to hold onto that malarial myth was his way of holding onto his years in Africa. It was his way of clinging to the past and to his youth when he had contracted it.

I visited Professor Lassene at his office on campus. I entered the dark, almost mystic room and took the familiar place in the leather chair in the corner. Professor Lassene told me he would retire at the end of the year.

"Professor Emeritus," he said. "Oh, I'll check in from time to time. But it won't be the same. In a sense I'm off to pasture."

I told him about what had happened at La Purísima.

"Now you know," he said. "You had to see it with your own eyes."

"But my mind still isn't settled about Martín's death. I know it wasn't an accident," I said.

"Sometimes deception may be the greater good. Perhaps to save the town and further generations, the priest's deception is what was best and warranted. It was done for the greater good," he said.

"What I learned in La Purísima is that sometimes it's impossible just to be an observer and a documenter," I told him. "That isn't life. And somewhere I crossed the line. At some point in La Purísima I strayed."

"Your profession is to be an observer," the professor said. "A chronicler... a documenter. But your profession and your life are not the same thing," he explained. I looked into his face, nearly hidden by the room's shadows. Then he asked:

"Were you in Mexico as an observer and for your

profession? Or were you there for other reasons or motives?"

"I struggle with the boundary—the boundary between life and profession. It's often hazy and unclear," I said. I was holding the final draft of the dissertation in my lap. I grasped it. "There is nothing in here about La Purísima, nothing about my trip to Mexico. None of that belongs here."

"I think you have your answer," he said.

What drew me to La Purísima was my friendship with Germán and the nagging mystery of Martín, like the rhythmic slamming of a hammer on a nail. His story is what I really went to hear. And too, to understand what drives people from their home. In the end I heard the story from Martín's lips and then helped bury him. Nothing was collected for the dissertation and I think that is best. I wouldn't want it another way.

Salvador was in my mind. A man, especially a man with a suspended mind couldn't be held accountable. At least not like other men. Salvador cannot be punished for loyalty. In La Purísima there is no law, at least no visible presence or formal institution. There was a different law, man's law, and perhaps justice too. For Martín, I don't know.

Where law doesn't exist, man will create it. Invariably, it will be imperfect like all of man's systems and institutions. In La Purísima law formed quickly and someone's justice was swiftly carried out. Whose justice? Not Martín. Germán? La Purísima? Father Gabriel? Laws are in place to protect people of a civilized society. What kind of place has no laws? A lawless, backward place, or perhaps a chaste village that never required law?

I set the dissertation on the professor's desk.

XX

Over the remaining weeks of summer I saw Jennifer a couple of times. Once I noticed her walking with friends by the lakefront, enjoying one of the last warm days of the year. She looked happy as she smiled and bounced along. She didn't notice me and I made no effort to speak with her. I saw her one other time at a restaurant we used to go to together. It was a little French bistro on Halsted. There was a new associate professor in the department and I was tasked with taking him to dinner one evening. Jennifer and I noticed one another across the room. She was with a man, a date I presumed. It was a little awkward to see her again and especially with someone else. Neither of us made any attempt to speak. Jennifer was too proud.

For a while I would still frequent some of the same restaurants we went to together. But that began to fade and soon I found different places that were closer to my apartment. Places that I could call my own. The café crawls continued. I still sought adventure in the unfamiliar, dank café, reading a novel, surrounded by a peculiar motif.

When autumn came I fell back into my routine of teaching. I was researching full-time faculty positions. I would have my doctorate by the end of the year and was anxious for a position starting at the beginning of the next. My sights were set on a position on the East Coast. As time passed, I thought less and less about Germán, Martín, and La Purísima. But I found myself wondering about Jesús and his life in Michigan. The orchards would be deserted now, asleep until next spring. Alternatively, La Purísima would be full again with its young men returned home for the winter. I imagined the place alive again with people strolling the plaza out front of the crumbling church, and Germán and Hortencia promenading hand in hand through the streets. Father Gabriel must feel pride now, proud that peace once again reigned in his town.

One day in October I again made the drive to Michigan. I knew Jesús worked in a factory near Traverse City and I had the home address that Magnolia had given me. It was one of those crystal clear autumn days with a blue sky that make you happy just to be under it. The air was crisp and the leaves were golden and fire orange, and all shades of red. And as autumn, vermilion days are intended, I wore a faded burgundy sweatshirt with University of Chicago printed on the front. I drove straight through despite those sleepy, harbor towns pulling me as I passed. They urged me to stop and gaze out into the lake and admire the red lighthouse. But I knew better and kept driving.

I found my way to the town and drove slowly through the handsome avenues searching for Garden Street. It was a college town. The small campus was scattered near a park and throughout wide residential streets.

Brick homes sat a distance from the curb atop grassy yards. Each lawn was strewn with leaves the color of autumn – rusts and yellows. A pile of leaves smoked in one yard and children played along the sidewalks while fat black squirrels gathered nuts for the winter. Church bells rang in the brick-lined town square. I thought what a wonderful town Jesús had selected. I thought of the boys, the *machitos* as Jesús called them. I pictured them happy, dashing and playing along these golden streets. I felt an effusion of happiness, almost euphoria wash over me. And then I came to Garden Street. Suddenly everything changed.

The euphoria that had stirred so quickly left me like air escaping a punctured balloon. There were empty lots scattered with garbage and an abandoned, boarded up house. At the end of the street were two apartment buildings, years ago painted gray but now the paint was peeling. The buildings were badly in need of repair. I went into the one where Jesús lived. In front of me lay a long dark hallway. There should have been lights along the corridor, but the bulbs were burned out. With straining eyes I read the apartment numbers on the doors. Below one peephole was a sticker of the Virgin of Guadalupe; it must be the place. I could hear Spanish being spoken, drifting from beneath the nearby doorways. I knocked. Jesús came to the door. At first, in the hallway's darkness, he didn't recognize me. Then the light from the apartment found me, or his eyes adjusted.

"*Maestro*! Come in!" he finally said, surprised, and we quickly embraced and slapped backs. Jesús worked the second shift at the factory and would have to leave soon for work. We sat at the table. I asked him how things were.

"Is it what you had hoped for?" Jesús looked down and contemplated his hands.

"No, *maestro*," he admitted."It isn't what I had imagined. We will have to return to Mexico."

"Why?"

"Dulce and the *machitos* aren't happy here. The school is difficult for Samuel and many of the boys here are rough. They are boys from Mexico too. Samuel has been in several fights. He was never like that in La Purísima. He was always a good boy," Jesús explained. "It's the stress of change."

"Have you made friends?" I asked.

"Sure. Most all the men in these apartments work at the factory or others nearby. They all come from different places in Mexico. But none from La Purísima." I asked about the job.

"Well, it's different," he confessed with shame or embarrassment. "There is no sunlight in the factory and it's dark. The work is boring. Sometimes I feel like I can't breathe, *maestro*. I feel like I have to go outside to get air."

After visiting La Purísima and its open spaces, I could understand. The conditions would be stifling for a man like Jesús.

"I think it can kill a man," he said. "At least his spirit."

"Isn't that all a man has?" I asked. "His spirit and his will?" Jesús agreed.

"I didn't think it would be like this," he admitted. "Maybe my dream was a bad one."

"No dreams are bad," I told him. "Dreams and reality

are different sometimes. That's all."

We talked about La Purísima. He told me that Germán and Hortencia were engaged to marry. From what he said, the people were happy now.

"Do you want to meet the boys?" he asked.

"Of course, I have heard so much about them."

He called down a narrow hallway. "Dulce!"

A woman and two small boys came hesitantly from a back bedroom. Dulce was like her picture. She was petite, had a round, ruddy face and I could see why he would sometimes call her his little square. At first the boys clung to their mother's skirt, but soon grew brave and we were talking. Samuel spoke of school and his friends, all of whom were Mexican immigrants.

I quickly learned that the cliques in school are sharply segregated. Samuel was reluctant to say negative things in front of his father. Pepito was little and his eyes were as black as any I had ever seen. He followed his older brother like a mirror's reflection. Jesús had to leave for work. We said our goodbyes, but he wanted me to stay a little longer. Jesús wanted me to know his boys.

The boys pulled chairs to the table. Samuel folded his arms and rested them on the tabletop and looked at me through serious, slanted eyes. Pepito did the same.

"Do you like things here?" I asked. They were quiet and looked at each other for a moment. Samuel shook his head.

"Why not?" He shrugged. Dulce walked up behind her oldest son and placed a hand on his shoulder, perhaps to give him the courage to tell me.

"Everything is different," he said. "I miss La

Purísima."

"Well, that's your home," I reminded him.

"But *papá* wanted it so bad. He wanted to make a life here," he said in a sudden burst of words. "But now we have to return to Mexico."

"Do you want to go back?"

"Yes. But I don't think I should be happy to go back," he said. "I feel happy and then I get angry at myself, like it's bad to be happy about leaving here."

"But if that's what you want..." I started.

"Maybe it's my fault," he admitted and started to cry. Tears streamed down the boy's face. He spoke between sobs, "*Papá* told us never to look over our shoulder. He told us never to look back. But I never stopped looking. Not for a minute." He turned to his mother and buried his head in her skirt.

"We knew it was his dream," Dulce said. "But such a difficult one."Samuel quieted.

"We tried hard," Dulce said. "All of us did. Really," she said as if convincing me. I said that I understood, and maybe I did.

"What do you miss most about La Purísima?" I asked Samuel. He cocked his head to one side, squinted, and looked to the ceiling.

Finally he answered, "the cows," as he wiped the final tear away. "I miss herding them. Oh, and I miss not having to wear shoes. At the little ranch I can run barefoot along the field and down to the river. Pepito and I like to wade in the cool water," he said excitely. Pepito smiled big.

"I know the river," I told them. "I have visited your home in Mexico." Both of the boys' eyes grew large in disbelief. "It's true," I told them smiling. They asked me things to make sure, to test me. They asked about their Aunt Magnolia and Uncle Salvador, about the river, and about Father Gabriel. They believed me, yet seemed amazed by it. They were connected to me because I knew La Purísima. For a time they forgot about their father's shattered dream. We laughed together. They didn't want me to leave when I did.

When I left I thought of the boy, Claudio, whom I had met in Morelia. The *machitos* would never have his advantages. By now it was late afternoon and the temperature had dropped. The sky was overcast, dark gray and misty. I left the town behind and on the way I passed through the orchards. The acres of trees were dormant and still. I pulled into the gravel drive where I used to meet with Germán and the others. Despite the cold air I parked and wandered a distance from the car. All I could see were endless rows of cherry trees, scraggly and bare. They would sleep until the spring. And the ground was hard earth, just matted dirt and faded grass.

It started to flurry. Not really snow, but the sky was spitting. Tiny white flakes fell around me and clung to my ears and sent a shiver through my body. I thought of the men gathered in a circle, talking and laughing. In their eyes was fatigue from work and a careless, but determined glimmer— a generation redefined. This happens when a poor country sleeps beside a rich one. Men come to work and to survive. *Not for your culture and not for your history.* What the men longed for was their return and I somehow felt the same. At least in spirit, what we long for is our home, the familiar, our loves, and *las morenas* with dusky skin and full lips and black eyes. I'll remember La Purísima.

I stared off through the leafless trees and the thin, whip-like branches. I felt as empty as the orchard. Yet I knew it would live again, in the spring, when the men of La Purísima return. They will come in droves, eager for the harvest. But now, only the long winter lay before me—just the cold and the gray.

Printed in the United States
202690BV00002B/235-240/A